A COOK'S GUIDE TO

ITALIAN
INGREDIENTS

A COOK'S GUIDE TO
ITALIAN
INGREDIENTS

KATE WHITEMAN

HERMES HOUSE

First published in 1999 by Hermes House

HERMES HOUSE books are available for bulk purchase for sales promotion and for premium use. For details, write or call the sales director: Hermes House, 27 West 20th Street, New York, NY 10011; (800) 354-9657

© Anness Publishing Limited 1999

Hermes House is an imprint of
Anness Publishing Inc.

ISBN 1 84038 205 8

Publisher: Joanna Lorenz
Senior Editor: Linda Fraser
Designer: Siân Keogh
Photographer: Janine Hosegood
Editorial Reader: Joy Wotton
Production Controller: Joanna King

Printed and bound in Singapore

1 3 5 7 9 10 8 6 4 2

Contents

Foreword

Italian cooks have traditionally relied on local ingredients – whatever could be gathered, cultivated or reared locally. Today, our supermarkets and delicatessens are full of these flavorful, good-quality ingredients. This comprehensive guide provides essential information on the huge range of Italian foods and shows you how to prepare and cook them.

Introduction

Italian cooking reflects the fact that the country was unified only in 1861. Until then, each region produced its own characteristic cuisine, relying exclusively on ingredients that could be gathered, cultivated or reared locally. Nowadays, of course, regional produce can be easily transported all over the country, but Italians still prefer to base their cooking on local ingredients, because they regard quality and freshness as more important than diversity and innovation. So the most flavorful sun–ripened tomatoes, eggplants and bell peppers are still found in the south, the freshest seafood is available along the coast, the finest hams come from the area where the pigs are raised, and so on. *La cucina italiana* remains distinctly regional; northern Italian cooking, for example, incorporates ingredients that are simply never found in the recipes of Sicily and Naples, and vice-versa. In the dairy-farming north, butter is used in place of the olive oil so prevalent in the south; bread and polenta are eaten instead of pasta. The only unifying feature is the insistence on high quality ingredients. Good food has always been essential to the Italian way of life. *La cucina italiana* is one of the oldest cooking cultures in the world, dating back to the Ancient Greeks and perhaps even earlier. The Romans adored food and often ate and drank to excess; it was they who really laid the foundations of Italian and

ITALIAN COOKS PREFER TO USE FRESH, GOOD QUALITY INGREDIENTS, SUCH AS JUICY, TART LEMONS, FRESHLY PICKED GLOBE ARTICHOKES, CRISP GREEN BEANS AND THE ESSENTIAL GARLIC TO MAKE SIMPLE, YET FLAVORFUL, DISHES.

European cuisine. The early Romans were peasant farmers who ate only the simple, rustic foods they could produce, such as grain, cheeses and olives. For them, meat was an unheard-of luxury; animals were bred to work in the fields and were too precious to eat. Trading links with other parts of the world, however, encouraged Roman farmers to cultivate new vegetables and fruits and, of course, grapes, while their trade in salt and exotic spices enabled them to preserve and pickle all kinds of meat, game and fish. Food became a near-obsession and ever more elaborate dishes were devised to be served at the decadent and orgiastic banquets for which the Romans were famed. The decline and fall of the Roman Empire led inevitably to a deterioration in the quality of cooking and a return to simple, basic foods. For centuries, regional cuisine reverted to its original uncomplicated style. With the Renaissance, however, came great wealth and a new interest in elaborate food. Once again, rich families strove to outdo each other with lavish banquets where courses of rich, extravagant foods were served—truffles, song–birds, game, desserts dripping with honey and spices—all washed down with vast quantities of wine. The poor, of course, continued to subsist on the simple foods they had always eaten, but the wealthier middle classes developed a taste for fine foods and created their own bourgeois dishes. The finer features of Italian cooking even reached the French, when Catherine de' Medici went to Paris to marry the future Henri II, taking fifty of her own cooks with her. They introduced new ingredients and cooking techniques to France and in return learned the art of French cuisine. In those regions of Italy that border France, you can still find reciprocal influences of French classical cooking but, generally speaking, Italians do not like elaborately sauced dishes, preferring to let the natural flavors of their raw ingredients speak for themselves.

EVEN TODAY, ALTHOUGH PRODUCE CAN BE TRANSPORTED QUICKLY AND EASILY ALL OVER THE COUNTRY, ITALIANS STILL RELY ON FRESH REGIONAL FOODS, SO THE MOST FLAVORFUL SUN-RIPENED TOMATOES (ABOVE), BELL PEPPERS (BELOW) AND EGGPLANTS (LEFT) ARE STILL FOUND – AND USED – MAINLY IN THE SOUTH.

The essence of Italian cooking today is simplicity. The Italian way of cooking fish is a good example of this. In coastal areas, freshly caught fish are most often simply grilled over hot coals, then served with nothing more than a splash of extra virgin olive oil, a wedge of lemon and freshly ground black pepper. Recipes such as *carpaccio di tonno*, in which the fish is so delicious raw that cooking seems unnecessary, and *branzino al forno*, where the delicate flavor of fennel is used to complement rather than obscure the fresh taste of the fish, are typically simple, as is *grigliata di calamari*, squid grilled with chilies to reflect its robust character.

Italians learn to appreciate good food when they are young children, and eating is one of the major pleasures of the day, no matter what the day of the week or time of the year. Witness an Italian family gathered around the Sunday lunch table in a local restaurant, and consider how the Italian menu of *antipasto* followed by pasta, rice or gnocchi, then fish, meat and vegetables served in sequence is devised so that each can be savored separately—both the food and the occasion are to be enjoyed as long as possible. The first course, or *antipasto*, is a unique feature. In restaurants, this can be a vast array of different dishes, both hot and cold, from which diners can choose as few or as many as they wish. At home with the family, it is more likely to be a slice or two of *salame* or *prosciutto crudo* with fresh figs or melon, if these are in season. But no matter how humble or grand the setting or the occasion, the *antipasto* is always visually tempting. Colorful dishes, such as *bruschetta casalinga* and *peperoni arrostiti con pesto*, are typical in this way.

The variety and diversity of the Italian ingredients available at supermarkets and delicatessens will surely inspire you to concoct any number of delicious meals, from a simple dish of pasta to a full-blown four-course dinner. A plate of *antipasto* followed by pasta or risotto flavored with seasonal ingredients, then simply cooked meat or fish and finally a local cheese and fruit makes a veritable feast. You could prepare a different meal along these lines every day of the year and almost never repeat the same combination. If you visit Italy, avail yourself of the local ingredients to prepare a menu full of the flavors of the region. Every area has its own special delights that make cooking a real pleasure.

FOR CENTURIES, ITALIAN COOKS HAVE BEGUN THEIR MEALS WITH SIMPLE ANTIPASTO LIKE THIS COLORFUL PLATTER OF FRESHLY COOKED VEGETABLES SERVED WITH A GARLICKY AIOLI AND RICH-TASTING OLIVE TAPENADE (ABOVE).

EVEN TODAY, TASTY, UNCOMPLICATED RECIPES STILL FORM THE BASIS OF ITALIAN REGIONAL CUISINE. HERE FRESH SALAD LEAVES AND HERBS (LEFT) ARE TOSSED WITH WALNUTS AND GORGONZOLA TO MAKE A LIGHT LUNCH-TIME SALAD TO SERVE WITH BRUSCHETTA: CHUNKY ROUNDS OF BREAD TOPPED WITH TOMATOES, CHEESE AND HERBS AND BROILED UNTIL HOT AND CRISP.

Pasta

If there is one ingredient that sums up the essence of Italian cooking, it must surely be pasta, that wonderfully simple and nutritious staple that can be formed into an almost infinite variety of shapes and sizes. In Italy, pasta is an essential part of every full meal and does not constitute a meal on its own. Il primo, *as the pasta course is called, is eaten between the* antipasto (appetizer) and il secondo (the main course). *Sometimes small pasta shapes are served in soup as* pasta in brodo. *There are two basic types of pasta,* pastasciutta (dried) and pasta fresca (fresh).

Today pasta is almost always factory-made. The dough is made from hard durum wheat, which produces an elastic dough, ideal for shaping into literally hundreds of different forms, from long, thin spaghetti to elaborate spirals and frilly, bow-shaped *farfalle*. Basic pasta dough is made only from durum wheat and water, although it is sometimes enriched with eggs (*pasta all'uovo*), which add an attractive yellow tinge, or colored and flavored with ingredients such as spinach (*pasta verde*) or squid ink (*pasta nera*). These traditional flavorings are more successful than modern gimmicky creations such as chocolate-flavored pasta. (Most Italians would throw up their hands in horror at this unauthentic folly.) Dried pasta has a nutty flavor and should always retain a firm texture when cooked. It is generally used for thinner-textured, more robust sauces.

Fresh pasta is usually made by hand, using superfine plain white flour enriched with eggs. Unlike dried pasta dough, it can be easily kneaded and is very malleable. Fresh pasta is often wrapped around a stuffing of meat, fish, vegetables or cheese to make ravioli, tortelli or cappelletti, or layered with sauce and meat or vegetables, as in lasagne.

Commercially made fresh pasta is made with durum wheat, water and eggs. The dough is harder than that used for handmade pasta, but it can be easily kneaded by machine. The flavor and texture of all fresh pasta is very delicate, so it is best suited to more creamy sauces.

HISTORY

The argument about the origins of pasta will probably rage on forever; the Chinese claim that they were the first to discover the art of noodle-making and that pasta was brought to Italy by Marco Polo. The Italians, of course, claim it as their own invention. Historians tell us that the Romans and probably even the Ancient Greeks used to eat pasta. Certainly the climate of southern Italy was ideally suited to growing durum wheat, so this theory is quite likely, but the popularity of pasta really spread in the fourteenth century, when bakeries in southern Italy started to sell pasta as an alternative to bread.

Then, as now, pasta was the traditional *primo* of the south, although in the poorest areas it constituted a complete meal. Its popularity filtered up to the north of Italy, and by the nineteenth century huge factories had been set up to mass-produce vast quantities of pasta, which quickly became an integral part of all Italian cooking.

BUYING AND STORING

Always buy dried pasta made from Italian durum wheat. Even after the package has been opened, dried pasta will keep for weeks in an airtight container. Handmade fresh pasta will keep only for a couple of days, but it can be successfully frozen. Machine-made fresh pasta is pasteurized and vacuum-packed, so it will keep in the refrigerator for up to two weeks and can be frozen for up to six months. When buying colored and flavored pasta, make sure that it has been made with natural ingredients.

COOKING PASTA

Allow about 3 oz pasta per serving as a first course. All pasta must be cooked in a large saucepan filled with plenty of salted, fast-boiling water.

For long shapes like spaghetti, drop one end of the pasta into the water and, as it softens, push it down gently until it bends in the middle and is completely immersed.

Cooking times vary according to the type, size and shape of the pasta, but, as a general rule, filled pasta takes about 12 minutes, dried pasta needs 8–10 minutes and fresh pasta only 2–3 minutes. All pasta should be cooked al dente, *so that it is still resistant to the bite. Always test pasta for doneness just before you think it should be ready; it can easily overcook. To stop the cooking, take the pan off the heat and run a little cold water into it, then drain the pasta.*

Preparing Fresh Pasta

1 Allow 1 egg to 3½ oz superfine plain flour. Sift the flour and a pinch of salt into a mound on a clean work surface and make a well. Break the eggs into the well and gradually work in the flour until completely combined.

2 Knead the dough with floured hands for at least 15 minutes, until it is very smooth, firm and elastic. (If you are short on time or energy, you can do this in a food processor.)

3 Chill the dough for 20 minutes, then roll it to the required thickness and cut it into your desired shape. (You can buy a specially shaped rolling-pin to make the squares for filled pasta.) A pasta machine will make this process much easier. Let the pasta dry for at least 1 hour before cooking it.

Pasta Varieties

Pasta shapes can be divided roughly into four categories: long strands and ribbons, flat, short and filled.

The best-known long variety is spaghetti, which comes in a thinner version, spaghettini, and the flatter *linguine*, which means "little tongues." *Bucatini* are thicker and hollow—perfect for trapping sauces in the cavity. Ribbon pasta is wider than the strands: Fettuccine, *trenette* and tagliatelle all fall into this category. Dried tagliatelle is usually sold folded into nests, which unravel during cooking. A mixture of white and green noodles is known as *paglia e fieno* (straw and hay). Pappardelle are the widest ribbon pasta; they are often served with s*ugo alla lepre* (hare sauce). The thinnest pasta strands are vermicelli (little worms) and ultra-fine *capelli d'angelo* (angel's hair).

In Italy, flat fresh pasta is often called *maccheroni*, not to be confused with the short tubes with which we are familiar. Lasagne and cannelloni are larger flat rectangles, used for layering or rolling around a filling; dried cannelloni are already formed into wide tubes. Layered pasta dishes such as this are cooked *al forno* (baked). Fillings for fresh pasta squares include meat, pumpkin, artichokes, ricotta and spinach, seafood, chicken and rabbit. There are dozens of names for filled pasta, but the only difference lies in the shape and size. Ravioli are square, tortelli are usually round, while tortellini and *anolini* are ring-shaped.

As for pasta shapes, the list is almost endless and the names wonderfully descriptive. There are *maltagliati* (badly cut), *orecchiette* (little ears) and *cappellacci* (bad hats), while from the natural world come penne (quills), *conchiglie* (little shells), *farfalle* (butterflies) and *lumache* (snails).

When choosing the appropriate pasta shape for the sauce, there are no hard and fast rules, but long, thin pasta is best for olive-oil-based and delicate seafood sauces. Short pasta shapes with wide openings (such as *conchiglie* and penne) will trap meaty or spicy sauces, as will spirals and curls. Almost any pasta is suitable for tomato sauce.

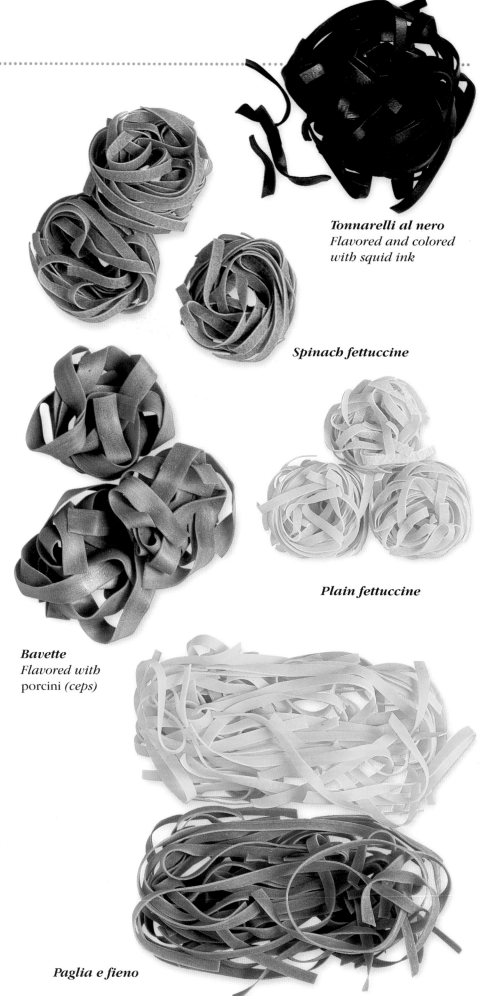

Tonnarelli al nero
Flavored and colored with squid ink

Spinach fettuccine

Plain fettuccine

Bavette
Flavored with porcini *(ceps)*

Paglia e fieno

Long Pasta

Fresh tomato, spinach and plain tagliatelle

Fresh tagliatelle Flavored with squid ink

Fresh spaghetti

Fresh paglia e fieno

Fresh tagliolini

Long Pasta

SPAGHETTI

INTEGRALE 100 % DI
FARRO
SPECIALITÀ
GASTRONOMICA

CASINO DI CAPRAFICO

AZIENDA AGRICOLA
GIACOMO SANTOLERI

500 g ℮

Farro spaghetti

TRADITIONAL ITALIAN
SPAGHETTI 1 Kg ℮

MADE BY:
PASTIFICIO
LUCIO GAROFALO s.p.a
GRAGNANO (NAPOLI)
ITALIA

**Long, plain
spaghetti**
*In Italy, still sold in
the traditional blue
paper roll*

Spaghetti tricolori
*Mixed plain, spinach
and tomato spaghetti*

Long, plain spaghetti

Linguine

Plain tagliatelle

Tagliatelle
*Flavored with
squid ink*

**Mushroom-flavored
tagliatelle**

Linguinette

Fettuccelle

Spinach tagliatelle

Long Pasta

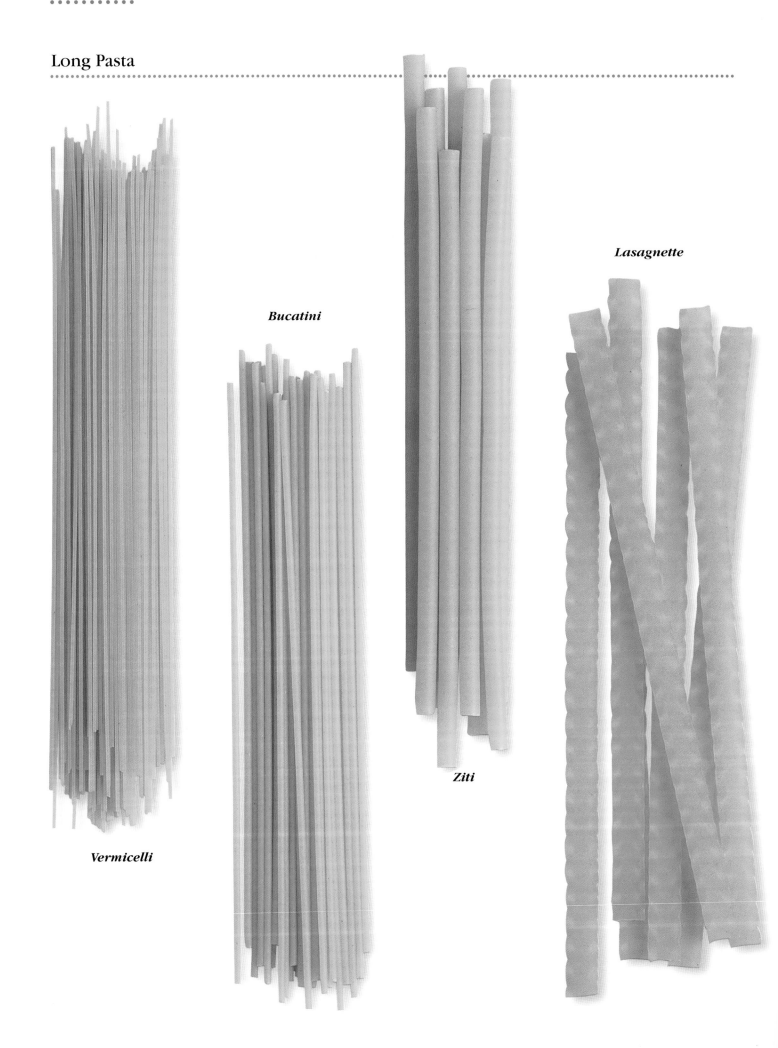

Vermicelli

Bucatini

Ziti

Lasagnette

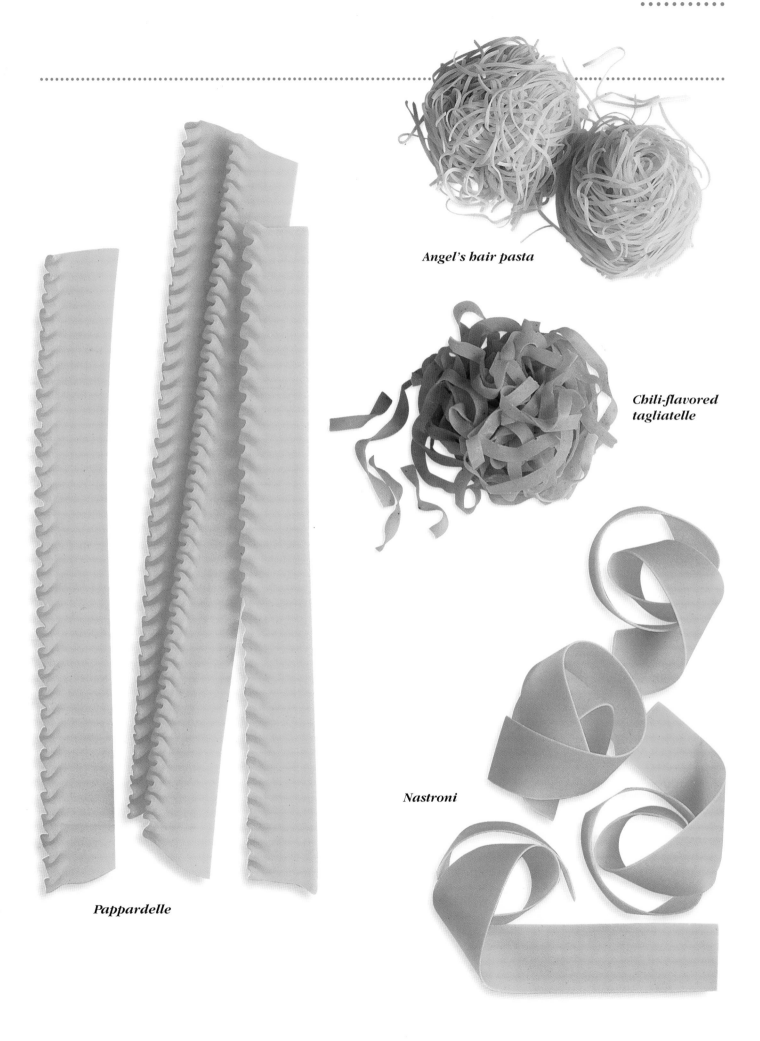

Angel's hair pasta

Chili-flavored tagliatelle

Nastroni

Pappardelle

Short Pasta

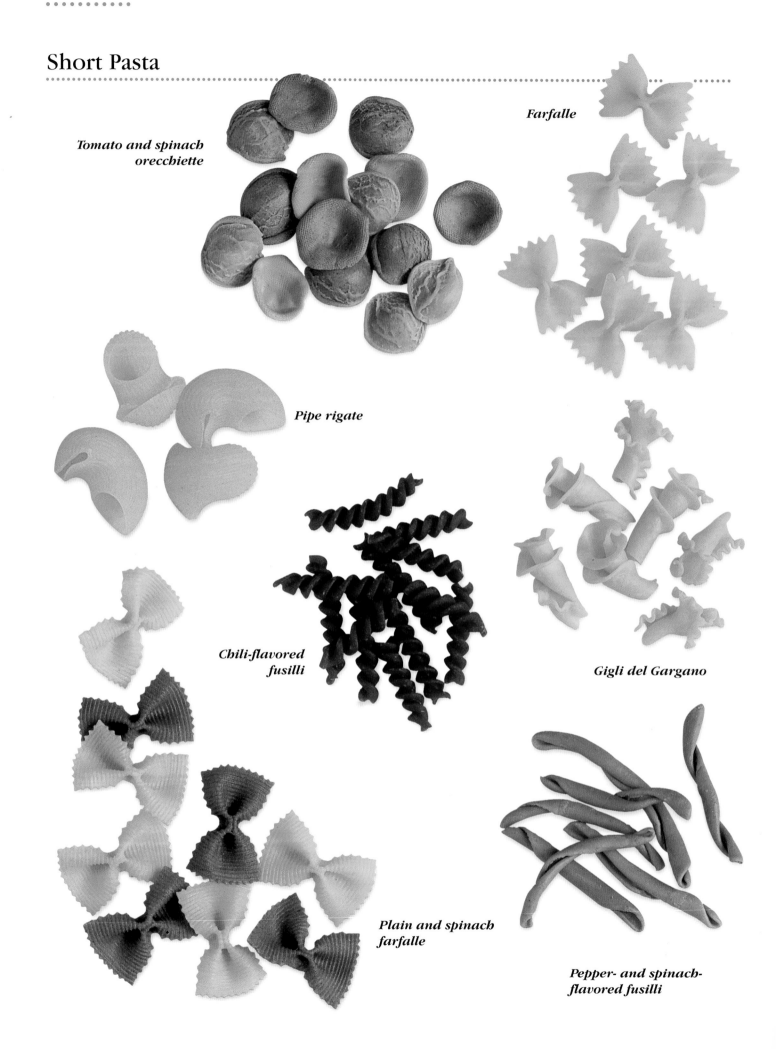

Tomato and spinach orecchiette

Farfalle

Pipe rigate

Chili-flavored fusilli

Gigli del Gargano

Plain and spinach farfalle

Pepper- and spinach-flavored fusilli

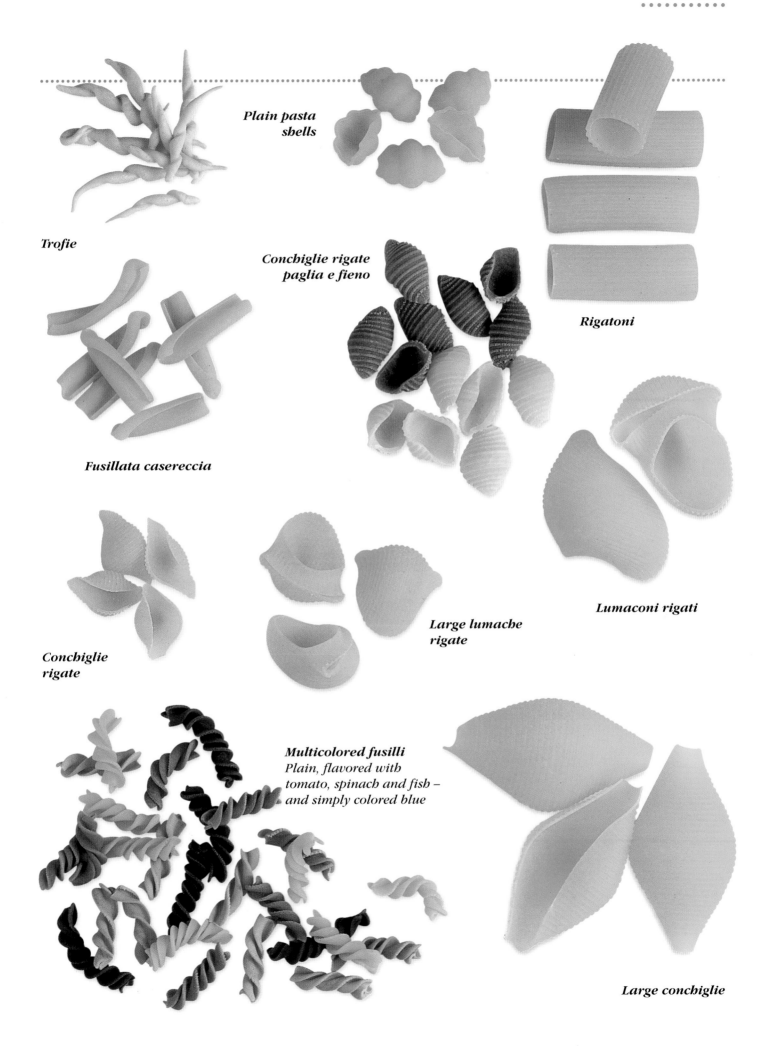

Plain pasta shells

Trofie

Conchiglie rigate paglia e fieno

Rigatoni

Fusillata casereccia

Conchiglie rigate

Large lumache rigate

Lumaconi rigati

Multicolored fusilli
Plain, flavored with tomato, spinach and fish – and simply colored blue

Large conchiglie

Short Pasta

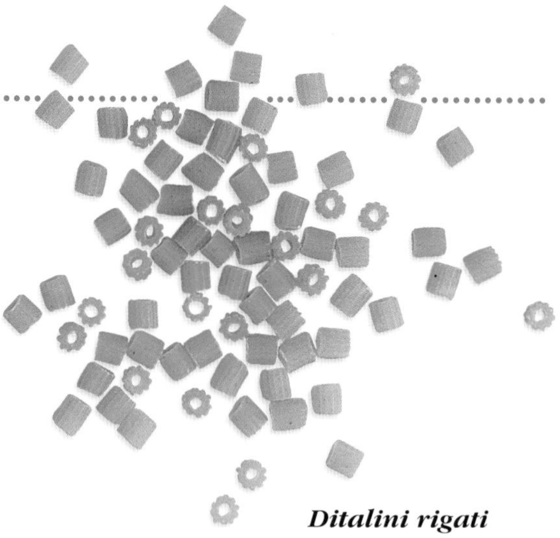

Ditalini rigati

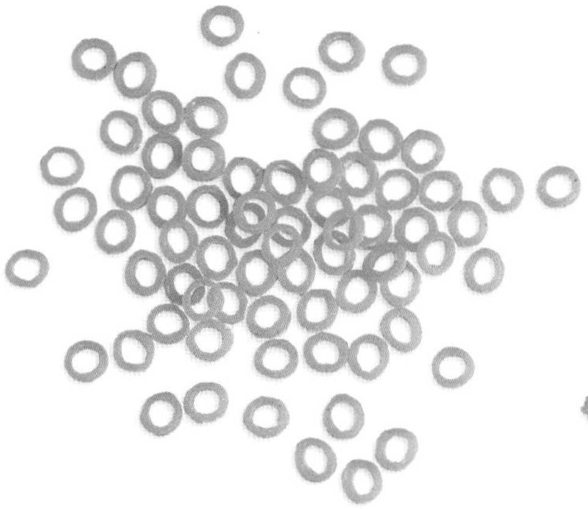

Anellini

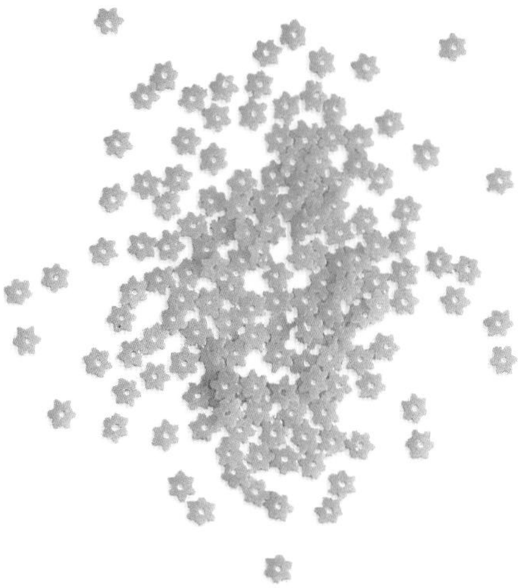

Stellette

Pennette rigate

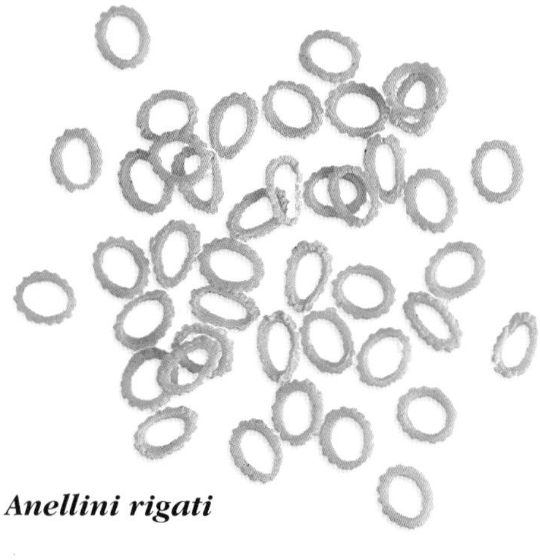

Anellini rigati

Fresh maccheroni rigati

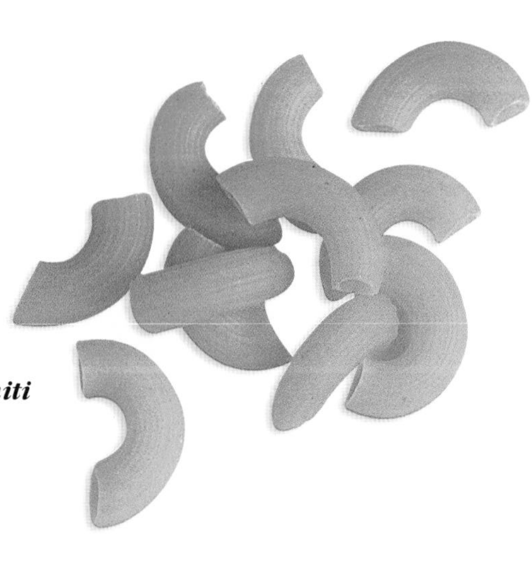

Gremiti

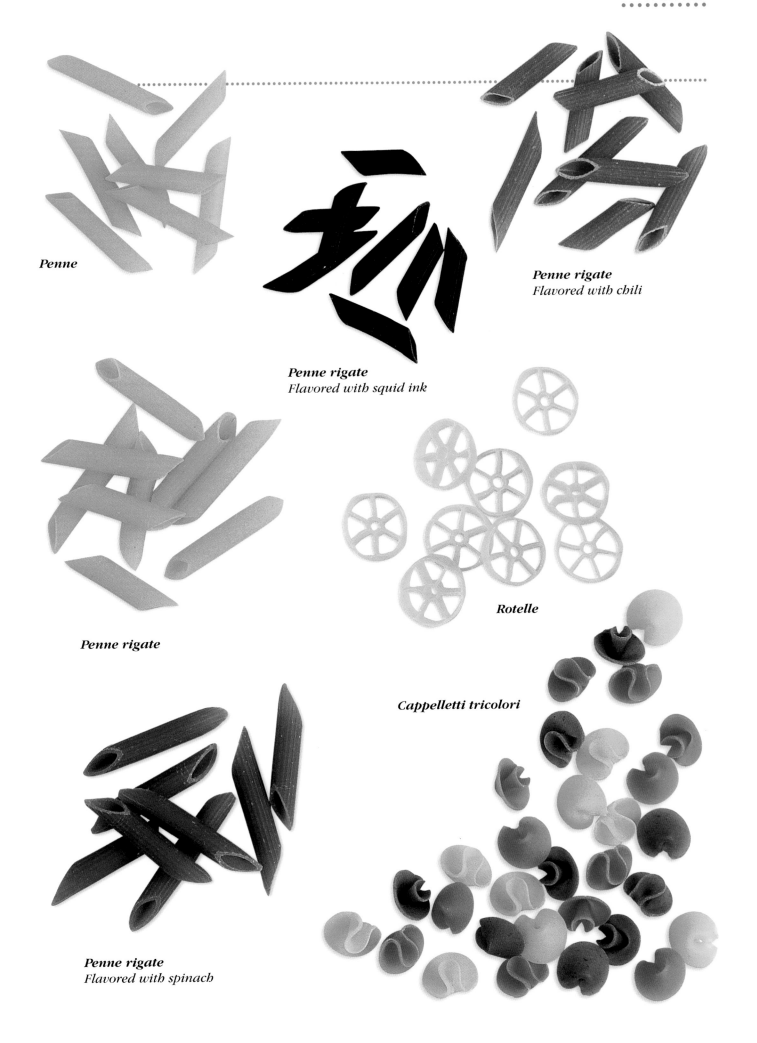

Penne

Penne rigate
Flavored with squid ink

Penne rigate
Flavored with chili

Penne rigate

Rotelle

Cappelletti tricolori

Penne rigate
Flavored with spinach

Flat Pasta

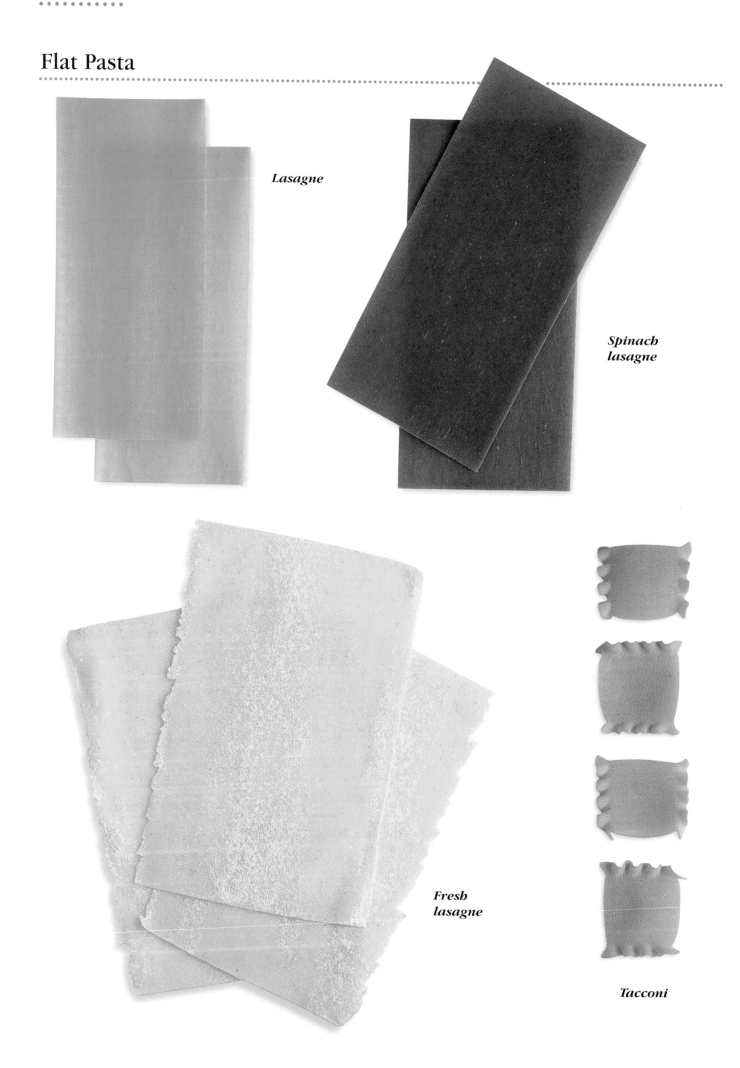

Lasagne

Spinach lasagne

Fresh lasagne

Tacconi

Filled Pasta

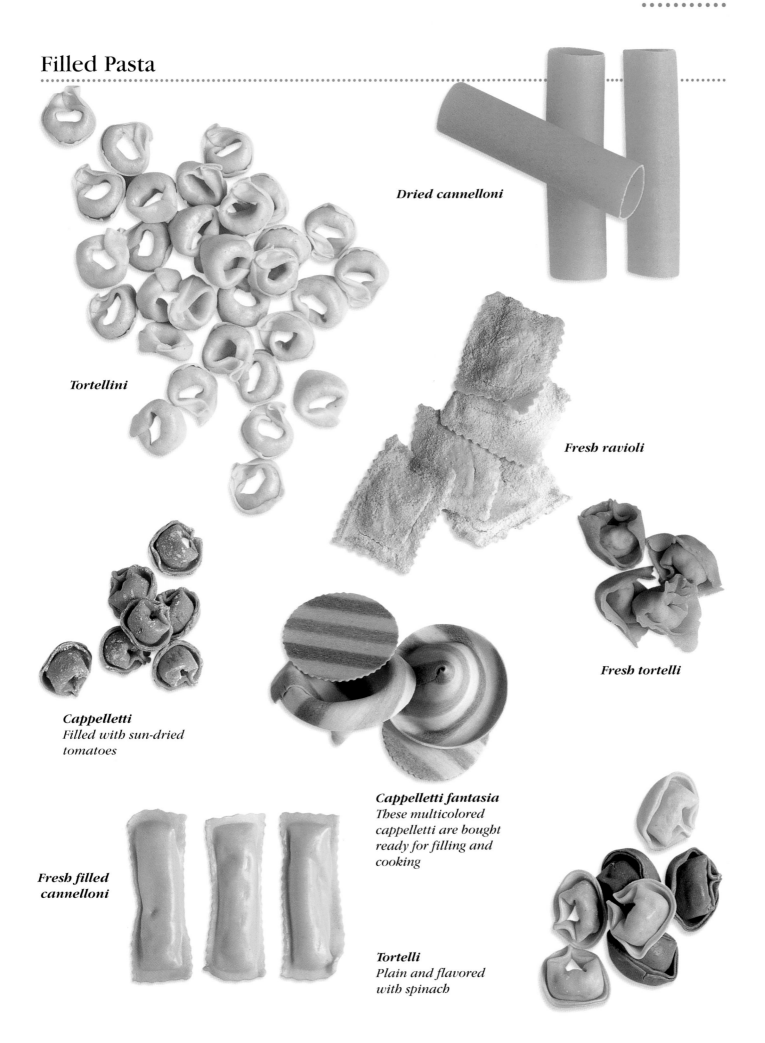

Dried cannelloni

Tortellini

Fresh ravioli

Cappelletti
Filled with sun-dried
tomatoes

Fresh tortelli

Cappelletti fantasia
These multicolored
cappelletti are bought
ready for filling and
cooking

**Fresh filled
cannelloni**

Tortelli
Plain and flavored
with spinach

Gnocchi

Gnocchi fall into a different category from other pasta, being more like small dumplings. They can be made with semolina (milled durum wheat), flour, potatoes or ricotta and spinach and may be shaped like elongated shells, ovals, cylinders or flat discs, or roughly shredded into *strozzapreti* (priest-stranglers); store-bought gnocchi are usually ridged ovals. However they are made, gnocchi should be extremely light and almost melt in the mouth.

CULINARY USES

Gnocchi can be served like any pasta, as a first course, in clear soup or occasionally as an accompaniment to the main course. Almost any pasta sauce is suitable for serving with gnocchi; they are particularly good with a creamy Gorgonzola sauce, or they can be served simply, drizzled with olive oil and dredged with freshly grated Parmesan.

BUYING AND STORING

Gnocchi are usually sold loose at better supermarkets. They are quite filling, so a small portion is enough for a first course; allow 4 oz per serving. They will keep in a ziplock bag in the refrigerator for two or three days. Homemade gnocchi dough will also keep for a couple of days before cooking.

COOKING GNOCCHI

With the exception of oven-baked gnocchi alla romana, all other types of gnocchi should be poached in a saucepan of lightly salted, barely simmering water.

Drop the gnocchi into the water in batches and cook for about 5 minutes; they will rise to the surface when they are done. Scoop out the cooked gnocchi with a slotted spoon and transfer to a plate: keep them warm while you cook the rest.

Fresh plain gnocchi

Gnocchi di patate

The best-known type of gnocchi are those from northern Italy made with potatoes and a little flour. To make 4 servings, peel 1¼ lb floury potatoes and boil until very tender. Drain and mash until smooth, then mix in 1 large egg and season with salt and pepper. Add 3½–4 oz flour, a little at a time, stirring well with a wooden spoon until you have a smooth, sticky dough that forms a ball on the spoon (you may not need all the flour). Turn out the dough onto a floured surface and knead for about 3 minutes, until soft and smooth. Cut the dough into 6 equal pieces and, with floured hands, roll these into sausage shapes about ¾ in in diameter. Slice the dough into ¾-in discs. Hold a fork in your left hand and press the discs against the tines just hard enough to make ridges, then flip them downward off the fork so that they curl up into elongated shell shapes. Poach them as above.

Fresh potato gnocchi

*Fresh spinach and
ricotta gnocchi*

*Fresh gnocchi made
with semolina*

Spinach and Parmesan gnocchi

Spinach and ricotta gnocchi

These attractive green gnocchi originated in Tuscany where, confusingly, they were known as ravioli. For 4 servings, you need:
12 oz cooked spinach, well
 drained and finely chopped
1 container (8 oz) ricotta, mashed
 until smooth
2 eggs
1 cup freshly grated
 Parmesan
3 tbsp flour
5 tbsp butter, melted
salt, pepper and nutmeg

1 Put the spinach, ricotta and seasoning in a saucepan and cook gently, stirring continuously, for 5 minutes. Off the heat, beat in the eggs, 3 tbsp of the Parmesan and the flour. Chill the mixture for at least 4 hours. Lightly shape into small rounds and roll them in a very little flour. Poach them as described, left.

2 Preheat the oven to 350ºF. Pour a little melted butter into a serving dish and put in the cooked gnocchi. Sprinkle with some of the remaining Parmesan and place in the oven.

3 Add the rest of the gnocchi as they are cooked and cover them with melted butter and Parmesan. Put the dish in the oven for another 5 minutes before serving.

Gnocchi alla romana

These substantial gnocchi from Lazio are made with semolina milled from durum wheat.
For 4–6 servings, you need:
4 cups milk
8 oz semolina
1 cup freshly grated Parmesan
2 eggs, plus an extra yolk,
 lightly beaten
5 tbsp butter
salt, pepper and nutmeg

1 Bring the milk to a boil, season with salt, pepper and nutmeg, then add the semolina in a steady stream, whisking for about 15 minutes, until the mixture is very thick. Off the heat, stir in half the Parmesan and the beaten eggs.

2 Pour the mixture into a greased baking tray to a thickness of about ¹/₂ in, or spread it over a dampened work surface. Let cool completely, then cut out 1¹/₄ in discs with a plain or fluted cookie cutter.

3 Preheat the oven to 350ºF. Layer the semolina discs in a buttered baking dish, dotting each layer with flakes of butter and a sprinkling of grated Parmesan, finishing with the cheese. Bake the gnocchi for about 15 minutes, until browned on top.

Rice, Grains & Beans

Almost as important as pasta in Italian cooking are rice, polenta and beans, which all appear as primi piatti *(first courses) in various guises. Like all basically agricultural countries, Italy relied heavily on these protein-rich ingredients when luxuries such as meat were in short supply, and a host of wholesome and delicious recipes were developed using these modest ingredients.*

Riso (Rice)

Italy produces more rice and a greater variety of rice than any other country in Europe. Most of it is grown in the Po Valley in Piedmont, where conditions are perfect for cultivating the short-grain Carnaroli, Arborio and *Vialone Nano* rice, which make the best risotto. Italian rice is classified by size, ranging from the shortest, roundest *ordinario* (used for puddings) to *semifino* (for soups and salads),

then *fino* and finally the longer grains of the finest risotto rice, *superfino*. *Superfino* rice swells to at least three times its original size during cooking, enabling it to absorb all the cooking liquid while still retaining its shape and firm *al dente* texture combined with a creamy smoothness.

HISTORY

The Saracens first introduced rice to Italy as long ago as the eleventh century (some believe even earlier), but it only became popular in the sixteenth century, when it began to be cultivated on a large scale in the Po Valley. Traditionally, rice has played a much greater part in the cooking of northern Italy than in the south, particularly in the Veneto, where the famous dish of *risi e bisi* (Venetian dialect for "rice and peas") opened the banquet served every year by the Doges to honor their patron Saint Mark.

Superfino Carnaroli rice **(left and above)**
This short-grained variety is one of the finest Italian rices. Its ability to absorb liquid and cook to a creamy smoothness while still retaining its shape makes it perfect for risotto

Arborio rice

Superfino Arborio rice

Vialone Nano rice

PREPARING RISOTTO

The most famous of all Italian rice dishes is risotto, which was invented in Milan in the sixteenth century. A good risotto can be made only with superfine rice. All risotti are basically prepared in the same way, although they can be flavored with an almost endless variety of ingredients. The rice is coated in butter or oil, then simmering stock is added, one ladleful at a time, and the rice is stirred over low heat until all the liquid has been completely absorbed.

Only then is more stock added, and the risotto is cooked in this way for about 20 minutes, until the rice is tender and creamy. The final touch is called mantecatura; *off the heat, a pat of butter or a couple of spoons of olive oil and some freshly grated Parmesan are stirred into the risotto to make it more creamy.*

Leftover risotto can be rolled into balls enclosing a piece of mozzarella, coated in fine bread crumbs and deep-fried to make supplì al telefono *or the Sicilian equivalent,* arancini.

Riso (Rice)

Rice is often used in Italian soups; it combines well with almost all vegetables and makes a substantial addition to minestrone. Baked rice dishes are also popular. Cooked rice is layered in a buttered ovenproof dish with meatballs, vegetables or poultry and cheese, then topped with bread crumbs and baked until the top is crispy and brown. The Italians never serve main dishes on a bed of rice, but prefer to serve plain boiled rice on its own with plenty of butter and cheese stirred in.

Buying and Storing

Buy only special superfine risotto rice for use in Italian cooking. Shorter grain *semifino* is best for soups, and *ordinario* for puddings (try *riso nero*, a rice pudding topped with melted chocolate). Once you have opened the package, reseal it tightly; you can then keep the rice in a dry place for several months.

Semifino rice

Brown semifino rice

Supplì al telefono

These rice croquettes contain mozzarella, which, when cooked, melts into strings that resemble "telephone wires." For 4 servings, you will need:

2 eggs, lightly beaten
8 oz cold, cooked risotto
6 oz prosciutto, cut into
  ¹/₂-in dice
4 oz mozzarella, cut into ¹/₂-in dice
fine dried bread crumbs,
  for coating
oil, for deep-frying
salt and freshly ground
  black pepper

1 Mix the eggs into the cold risotto and season to taste with plenty of salt and pepper.

2 Form the rice mixture into balls about the size of a small orange and make a hollow in each one. Fill this with a cube of ham and one of cheese, then roll each ball in your hand to enclose the ham and cheese completely, adding a little more rice if necessary.

3 Spread out the bread crumbs on a shallow tray or plate and roll the rice balls in the bread crumbs to coat them lightly.

4 Heat the oil in a deep, heavy pan and deep-fry the rice balls in batches for 3–5 minutes, until golden brown. Drain on paper towels and keep warm while you cook the remainder. Serve piping hot.

Farro

This is the Tuscan name for spelt, a hard brown wheat with pointed grains, which is rarely used in other parts of Italy. *Farro* is much harder than other wheat and therefore takes longer to process and cook, but it will grow even in poor soil. In Tuscany it is used to make *gran farro*, a delicious and nourishing soup, which is served as a first course instead of pasta.

CULINARY USES

Farro is used mainly as an ingredient for soups, but in remoter country areas of Italy it is sometimes used to make bread.

> **COOK'S TIP**
> *When cooking rice, a good rule of thumb is: The better the rice, the longer the cooking time required, so ordinario will need only 10–12 minutes' cooking compared with up to 20 minutes for superfino.*

> **COOK'S TIP**
> *Farro is a very hard grain and must be boiled for up to 3 hours to make it digestible before adding to other recipes. It can also be simply cooked and served with olive oil and freshly ground black pepper.*

Farro

Ordinario rice

Gran farro

This Tuscan soup is often served as a first course instead of pasta. For 4 servings, you will need:

8 oz dried borlotti or
  cannellini beans,
  soaked overnight, then drained
1 onion, chopped
2 garlic cloves, chopped
4 oz finely chopped *pancetta*
4 sage leaves
a pinch of chopped fresh
  oregano
3 tbsp olive oil
8 oz chopped fresh tomatoes
5 oz prepared *farro*
salt, freshly ground black pepper
  and grated nutmeg

1 Cook the beans in fresh water until tender (reserve the cooking water). Put the beans through a vegetable mill. Gently cook the onion, garlic, *pancetta* and herbs in the olive oil until pale golden brown. Add the tomatoes, season with salt, pepper and nutmeg, then simmer for 10 minutes.

2 Add the bean purée and enough of the cooking water to make a thick soup. Stir in the *farro* and simmer for 45 minutes, adding more water if the soup becomes too thick. Serve with some extra virgin olive oil to trickle into it.

Polenta

For centuries, polenta has been a staple food of the north of Italy, particularly around Friuli and the Veneto. This grainy yellow flour is a type of cornmeal made from ground maize, which is cooked into a kind of porridge with a wide variety of uses. Polenta is sometimes branded according to the type of maize from which it is made. *Granturco* and *Fioretto* are the two most common types.

In Italy, polenta is available ground to various degrees of coarseness to suit different dishes, but there are two main types—coarse and fine. Coarse polenta has a more interesting texture but takes longer to cook.

GRILLED OR FRIED POLENTA

Pour the cooked polenta onto a wooden board and spread it to a thickness of about 1 in. Let cool and harden, then cut into squares.

Fry in hot vegetable oil until crunchy and golden, then drain on paper towels or grill until golden brown on both sides.

To make a pasticciata *(layered baked dish) of polenta, cut the cold polenta horizontally into* $1/2$*-in slices and layer it in a buttered baking dish with your chosen sauce, mushrooms, cheeses, etc. Bake for about 15 minutes, until the top is lightly browned.*

HISTORY

The Romans made a savory porridge they called *puls* using *farro*, a kind of spelt, and the tradition continued in northern Italy, where gruels were prepared from local cereals such as buckwheat, barley and oats. Maize or corn was only introduced into Italy from the New World in the seventeenth century; soon it was being grown in all the northeastern regions, where cornmeal overtook all other types of grain in popularity, because it combined so well with the local dairy products. Traditionally, polenta was cooked in a *paiolo*, a special copper pot which hung in the fireplace; here, it was stirred for at least an hour, to be served for breakfast, lunch or dinner (sometimes all three).

CULINARY USES

Polenta is extraordinarily versatile and can be used for any number of recipes, ranging from rustic to highly sophisticated. Although it is most often served as a first course, it can also be used as a vegetable dish or main course and even made into cookies and cakes. Plain boiled polenta can be served on its own, or enriched with butter and cheese to make a very satisfying dish. It goes wonderfully well with all meats, sausages and game, helping to cut the richness and mop up the sauce. It can be cooled and cut into squares, then fried, grilled or baked and served with a topping or filling of mushrooms, meat, vegetables or cheese. Fried or grilled squares of polenta form the basis of *crostini*, which are served as an *antipasto*.

Fine polenta

BUYING AND STORING

It is possible to buy quick-cooking polenta, which can be prepared in only 5 minutes. However, if you can spare the 20 minutes or so that it takes to cook traditional polenta, it is best to buy this for its superior texture and flavor. Whether you choose coarse or fine meal is a matter of personal preference; for soft polenta or sweet dishes, fine-ground is better, while coarse-ground meal is better for frying. Once you have opened the bag, put the remaining polenta in an airtight container; it will keep for at least a month.

Coarse polenta

COOK'S TIP

Polenta can be cooked in water, stock or a mixture of water and milk. Whichever liquid you use, cook the polenta very slowly and steadily so that it does not become lumpy. Allow ¹/₂ cup polenta meal per person.

SWEET POLENTA FRITTERS

Polenta can be used to make sweet as well as savory dishes. To make enough fritters to serve four, combine 3 cups milk, 6 tbsp superfine sugar and a pinch of salt in a saucepan and bring to a boil. Add 5 oz polenta in a steady stream, stirring constantly for 20 minutes. Off the heat, stir in 2 tbsp butter, 3 egg yolks and the grated rind of 1 lemon and continue to stir for 1 minute. Spread out the polenta on a dampened baking sheet to a thickness of ¹/₂ in. When cold, cut into rectangles or diamonds. Coat lightly with fine dry bread crumbs, then deep-fry in hot oil until golden. Drain on paper towels and dust with confectioners' sugar before serving.

Recipe for Basic Polenta

To make a basic polenta for 4–6 people, bring 6 cups salted water or stock to a boil.

Gradually add 2 cups polenta in a steady stream, stirring continuously with a wooden spoon. Continue cooking, stirring constantly, until the polenta comes away from the sides of the saucepan. This will take 20–30 minutes (5 minutes for quick-cooking polenta).

One alternative, foolproof (though unauthentic) method is to put the polenta meal into a saucepan, add salt, then stir in the cold water, bring the mixture slowly to a boil and simmer gently for about 20 minutes, stirring occasionally.

Another is to cook the polenta on the stove for 5 minutes, then finish cooking it in the oven for an hour.

Pour the cooked polenta into a serving dish, season with pepper and stir in abundant quantities of butter and a strong-flavored cheese—Parmesan, Fontina, Bel Paese and Gorgonzola are all delicious with piping hot polenta.

Beans

Fagioli (beans)

Beans are another staple of Tuscan cooking; indeed, the Tuscans are sometimes nicknamed "the bean-eaters," although beans are eaten all over Italy. The most popular varieties include the pretty red-and-cream speckled borlotti, the small white cannellini (a kind of kidney bean), the larger *toscanelli* and *fagioli coll'occhio* (black-eyed beans). All these are eaten as hearty stews, with pasta and in soups, and cannellini are often served as a side dish simply anointed with extra virgin olive oil. *Ceci* (chickpeas) and *fave* (fava beans) are also popular.

HISTORY

Beans were a staple of the Roman and Greek diet, and several recipes for bean stews survive from that period. Many of the beans were brought to Italy from the Middle East, but some, such as *fave*, were indigenous and were used as ritual offerings to the dead at Roman funerals. Beans have always been a popular peasant food, but, during the Renaissance, Catherine de Medici attempted to refine Italian cuisine, and beans fell out of favor with the nobility and sophisticated urban dwellers. Thanks to their highly nutritious and economical qualities, however, beans and legumes have once again become an important element in Italian cooking.

CULINARY USES

Beans can be made into any number of nutritious soups and stews, or served as the basis of a substantial salad such as *tonno e fagioli* (tuna and beans). One popular Tuscan dish is *fagioli all'uccelletto* (beans cooked like little birds). Cooked cannellini beans are combined with chopped garlic, fresh sage leaves and tomatoes and simmered for about 15 minutes, until tender and fragrant. This dish is delicious served with coarse country sausages.

Dried red borlotti beans

Dried cannellini beans

Dried borlotti beans

Dried cannellini beans

Canned borlotti beans

Buying and Storing

During the summer and early autumn in Italy, you may find fresh beans, sometimes still in the pod. Borlotti beans come in an attractive speckled pod, cannellini in a slim yellowish pod. The pods represent a high proportion of the weight, so allow at least 12 oz per serving. Most beans, however, are sold dried. Try to buy these at a store with a quick turnover, or they may become shriveled and very hard. Prepackaged beans will have a "best before" date on the package. Loose beans will keep for several weeks in a cool, dry place, but are at their best soon after purchase.

If you don't have the time to prepare dried beans, canned varieties make an acceptable substitute, but you cannot control the texture and they are sometimes too mushy. They are, however, fine for recipes that call for puréed beans. Bear in mind, though, that they are an expensive alternative to dried beans.

Canned beans

Cooking Beans

All dried beans should be soaked for about 8 hours in cold water or 4 hours in boiling water before cooking (this is not necessary for fresh beans). Discard the soaking water before cooking the beans.

Cook the beans in plenty of unsalted boiling water. Boil briskly for 10 minutes (this is essential to kill off the toxins, which may cause severe stomachaches), then simmer for 1–2 hours, depending on the size and freshness of the beans.

You can add whatever flavorings you wish to the cooking liquid, but never add salt or any acidic ingredients, such as tomatoes or vinegar, until the beans are cooked, or they will never become tender however long you cook them. To make a hearty stew, after the initial boiling, the beans can be mixed with pancetta, garlic and herbs and cooked very slowly in the oven.

Canned cannellini beans

Canned black-eyed beans

Beans

Fave (fava beans)

Fava beans are best eaten fresh from the fat green pod in late spring and early summer when they are very small and tender with a bittersweet flavor. They are particularly popular in the area around Rome, where they are eaten raw with prosciutto, salami or Pecorino. Later in the season, they should be cooked and skinned (hold the hot beans under cold running water; the skin will slip off quite easily). Cooked *fave* have a milder flavor than raw and are excellent with ham and *pancetta*. When buying fresh *fave* in the pod, allow about 12 oz per person; it may seem a lot, but the

pods themselves are comparatively heavy, so a lot goes only a little way. Dried *fave* should be soaked, and the skins removed before cooking. They are used for soups and stews and need about 45 minutes' cooking.

Chickpeas
These round golden legumes can be bought dried (above), or canned and ready to use (left)

Broad beans
Dried fave *need to be soaked overnight before cooking*

Ceci (chickpeas)

These round golden legumes are shaped rather like hazelnuts and have a distinctive, nutty flavor. They are the oldest of all known legumes and, though not indigenous to Italy, have become very popular in Italian country cooking.

CULINARY USES

Chickpeas are cooked and used in the same way as beans and are an essential ingredient of *tuoni e lampi* (thunder and lightning), a sustaining dish of pasta and chickpeas served with tomato sauce and Parmesan. They can also be served cold, dressed with lemon juice, chopped fresh herbs and olive oil, to make a substantial salad.

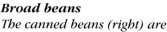

Broad beans
The canned beans (right) are ready to use

> ### COOK'S TIP
> *Chickpeas can be very hard, so it is best to soak them for at least 12 hours, then cook them in plenty of boiling water for up to 2 hours.*

Lenticchie (lentils)

Although lentils grow in pods, they are always sold podded and dried. Italian lentils are the small brown variety, which are grown in the area around Umbria; they do not break up during cooking and are often mixed with small pasta shapes or rice for a contrast of flavors and textures. They make the perfect bed for cooked sausage, such as zampone or cotechino, and are delicious served cold dressed with olive oil. The ultimate Italian legume feast must surely be *imbrecciata*, a nutritious and sustaining soup from Umbria made with chickpeas, beans and lentils.

Brown lentils
These are available in different sizes, large (below) and small (above)

COOK'S TIP
Lentils will absorb the flavors of whatever herbs they are cooked with, so add any appropriate herbs or spices to the cooking liquid.

Cheeses

Italy has an even greater variety of cheeses than France, ranging from fresh, mild creations, such as mozzarella, to aged, hard cheeses with a very mature flavor, such as Parmesan. All types of milk are used, including sheep's, goat's and buffalo's, which produces the best mozzarella, and some cheeses are made from a mixture of milks. As in France, the Italians eat their cheese after the main course, either accompanied or followed by fresh fruit. You will not, however, find the large selection of cheeses offered on a French menu; Italian restaurants serve only one or two types of cheese and rarely have a cheeseboard.

Many of the cheeses made in Italy are suitable for cooking. What would a pizza be without its delicious, stringy topping of melted mozzarella, or a pasta dish without a grating of fresh Parmesan?

HISTORY

Fresh, rindless cheeses were first introduced to Italy by the ancient Greeks, who taught the Etruscans their cheese-making skills. They in turn refined the craft, developing the first long-matured cheeses with hard rinds, which could last for many months and would travel well. Today's Parmesan and Pecorino cheeses are probably very similar to those produced 2,500 years ago.

In ancient days, the milk was left to curdle naturally before being made into cheese. The Romans discovered that rennet would speed up this process. Originally, they probably used rennet made from wild artichokes (this is still used in remoter parts of Italy), but later they began to use animal rennet. The process used to make farmhouse cheeses today has changed very little since Roman times.

Italian cheeses can be divided into four categories: hard, semi-soft, soft and fresh. Some cheeses have an enormously high fat content; others are low in fat and suitable for dieters. Many Italian cheeses are eaten at different stages of maturity; a cheese that has been matured for about a year is known as *vecchio*; after 18 months, it becomes *stravecchio* and tends to have a very powerful flavor. Almost all Italian cheeses can be eaten on their own and also used for cooking.

Hard Cheeses

Asiago

This cheese from the Veneto region develops different characteristics as it ages. The large round cheeses with reddish-brown rinds each weigh 22–55 lb. They are made from partially skimmed cow's milk and have a fat content of only 30 percent. Asiago starts life as a pale straw-colored dessert cheese, pitted with tiny holes, with a mild, almost bland flavor. After six months, the semi-matured cheese (*asiago da taglio*) develops a more piquant, saltier flavor, but can still be eaten on its own. Once it has matured for 12 to 18 months, the *stravecchio* cheese becomes grainy and sharp-tasting, resembling an inferior Grana Padano, and is really only suitable for grating and cooking.

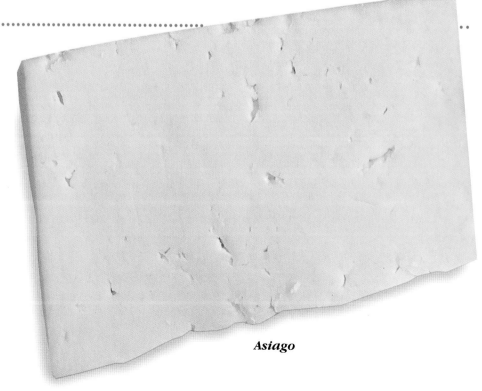

Asiago

Parmesan

Parmesan is by far the best-known and most important of the Italian hard cheeses. There are two basic types—Parmigiano Reggiano and Grana Padano—but the former is infinitely superior.

PARMIGIANO REGGIANO

Parmigiano Reggiano can be made only in a strictly defined zone, which lies between Parma, Modena, Reggio-Emilia, Bologna and Mantua. The farmers of this area claim that the cheese has been made there for over 2,000 years; certainly it appears to be almost identical to that produced by the Etruscans and the methods of production have scarcely changed. The milk comes only from local cows, which graze on the area's rich pastureland.

It takes about 132 gallons of milk to make one 70–80 lb wheel of Parmigiano Reggiano. The milk is partially skimmed and some of the whey from the previous day's cheese-making is added, then the mixture is carefully heated before rennet is added to encourage curdling. (The rest of the whey is fed to local pigs destined to become prosciutto) The curds are poured into wheel-shaped forms and the cheese is then aged for a minimum of two years; a really fine Parmesan may be aged for up to seven years. During this time, it is nurtured like fine wine, until it becomes pale golden with a slightly granular flaky texture and a nutty, mildly salty flavor. Authentic Parmigiano Reggiano has the word "Reggiano" stamped on the rind.

GRANA PADANO

This cheese is similar to Parmigiano Reggiano, but is inferior in flavor and texture. Although it is made in the same way, the milk used comes from other regions and the cheese is matured for no more than 18 months, so it does not have the crumbly texture of Reggiano and its flavor is sharper and saltier. Its grainy texture (hence the name "grana") makes it fine for grating and it can be used for cooking in the same way as Reggiano.

CULINARY USES

A really good Parmigiano Reggiano can be eaten on its own, cut into chunks or slivers; it is delicious served with ripe pears and a good red wine. But Parmesan, both Reggiano and grana, really comes into its own when used for cooking. Unlike other cheeses, it does not become stringy or rubbery when exposed to heat, so it can be grated over any number of hot dishes, from pasta, polenta and risotto to minestrone, or layered with eggplant slices or truffles and baked in the oven. Slivers of fresh Parmesan are also excellent with asparagus or in a crisp salad. Don't throw away the rind from Parmesan; use it to add extra flavor to soups and vegetable stocks.

Parmigiano Reggiano

Grana Padano

BUYING AND STORING

If possible, buy Parmigiano Reggiano, which is easily recognizable by the imprint "Reggiano" in pinpricks on the rind. Whether you buy Reggiano or grana, always buy it in a piece cut from a whole wheel and grate it freshly when you need it; if possible, avoid pre-packed pieces and never buy ready-grated Parmesan, which is tasteless. Tightly wrapped in foil, a hunk of Parmesan will keep in the refrigerator for at least a month.

Hard Cheeses

Pecorino

All Italian cheeses made from sheep's milk are known as Pecorino, but they vary enormously in texture and flavor, from soft and mild to dry and strong. The best-known hard Pecorino cheeses are *romano* from Lazio and *sardo* from Sardinia; both are medium-fat, salty-tasting cheeses with a sharp flavor, which becomes sharper the longer the cheeses are matured. The milder *sardo* is usually aged for only a few weeks; the *romano* for up to 18 months. Hard Pecorino is a pale, creamy color with a firm granular texture with tiny holes like Parmesan. Sicilian *pecorino pepato* is studded with whole black peppercorns, which add a very piquant note.

Fresh Pecorino comes from Tuscany and is sometimes known as *caciotta.* This semi-hard cheese has a delicious mild, creamy flavor, but is not easy to find outside Italy, as it keeps for a very short time.

History

Pecorino romano is probably the oldest Italian cheese, dating back to Roman times. Then, as now, the cheeses were shaped and laid on *canestri* (rush mats, rather like hammocks) to be air-dried. Sicilian Pecorino is still called *canestro* after these rush mats.

Culinary Uses

Hard Pecorino can be grated and used exactly like Parmesan. It has a more pungent flavor, which is well suited to spicy pasta dishes, such as *penne all'arrabbiata*, but it is too strong for more delicate dishes such as risotto or creamy chicken dishes. *Caciotta* can be cubed and marinated in olive oil for about 2 hours, then served with a grinding of black pepper to make a delicious and unusual *antipasto*.

Buying and Storing

Fresh or semi-hard Pecorino should be eaten the day you buy it, but well-matured Pecorino will keep in the refrigerator for several weeks wrapped tightly in foil.

Pecorino pepato
This cheese is studded with whole black peppercorns

Pecorino sardo
A milder version that is aged for only a few weeks

Caciotta
A semi-hard cheese with a mild, creamy flavor

Provolone

A southern Italian cheese, straw-white in color with a smooth, supple texture and an oval or cylindrical shape, Provolone comes in many different sizes (some enormous) and can often be found hanging from the ceiling in Italian delicatessens. Provolone can be made from different types of milk and rennet; the strongest versions use goat rennet, which gives them a distinctively spicy flavor. In the south of Italy, buffalo milk is often used, and the cheeses are sometimes smoked to make *provolone affumicato*. The cheese is made by the *pasta filata* (layering) process, which gives it a smooth, silky texture; the curds are left to solidify, then they are cut into strips before being pressed together into a sausage shape. This is salted in brine for 6 to 12 hours, then the cheese is shaped and left to mature.

Variations on Provolone include *caciocavallo*, a smooth smoky cheese made from a mixture of cow's and goat's or sheep's milk, which develops a sharp flavor that becomes sharper as it matures. It gets its name from the way the oval cheeses are tied up in pairs and hung up to dry over a wooden pole, as though on horseback. (One false theory is that the cheese was originally made from mare's milk; another is that the cheeses were stamped with a horse, which is the symbol of Naples.) In Calabria, a version called *burrino* is made enclosing a lump of unsalted butter in the center of the cheese, so that when it is sliced, it resembles a hard-cooked egg.

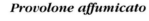

Provolone affumicato

Provolone burrino
There is a lump of butter buried in the center of this cheese, so that when cut it resembles a hard-cooked egg yolk

CULINARY USES

Milder fresh Provolone can be eaten on its own or in a sandwich with mortadella or ham. Once it becomes strong, it should only be used for cooking; its stringy texture when melted makes it ideal for pizzas and pasta dishes.

BUYING AND STORING

Enclosed in their wax rinds, Provolone and similar cheeses will keep for months. Once they have been opened, they should be eaten within a week. Provolone can be used for cooking in the same way as Parmigiano Reggiano.

Provolone

Provolone
Its stringy texture when melted makes this cheese particularly good for pizzas

Semi-hard Cheeses

Bel Paese

This cheese, poetically named "beautiful country," is a baby among Italian cheeses, having been created by the Galbani family from Lombardy early this century. Made from cow's milk, it contains over 50 percent fat, which makes it very creamy. It is the color of buttermilk, with a very mild flavor, and is wrapped in pale yellow wax to preserve its freshness. A whole Bel Paese weighs about 4¼ lb, but it is often sold pre-packaged in wedges.

CULINARY USES

Bel Paese can be eaten on its own; its mild creaminess makes it popular with almost everyone. It is also excellent for cooking, with a good melting quality, and can be used as a substitute for mozzarella, but because it is rather bland it will not add much flavor to a dish.

BUYING AND STORING

Like most cheeses, it is best to buy a wedge of Bel Paese cut from a whole cheese; pre-packaged pieces tend to be soggy and tasteless, although they are fine to use in cooking. Use freshly cut cheese as soon as possible after purchase, although wrapped in foil or plastic wrap it will keep in the refrigerator for two or three days.

Fontina

The only genuine Fontina comes from the Val d'Aosta in the Italian Alps, although there are plenty of poor imitations. True Fontina is made from the rich unpasteurized milk of Valdostana cows and has a fat content of 45 percent. Although today Fontina is produced on a large scale, the methods are strictly controlled and the cows are grazed only on alpine grass and herbs. Because it is matured for only about four months, the cheese has a mild, almost sweet, nutty flavor and a creamy texture, with tiny holes. Longer-matured Fontina develops a much fuller flavor and is best used for cooking. A whole Fontina weighs about 33–44 lb; the cheese is pale golden and the soft rind is orangey-brown. The rind of authentic Fontina has the words "Fontina dalla Val d'Aosta" inscribed in white writing.

HISTORY

Fontina has been made for at least 500 years; it is mentioned in the "dairy bible" *La Summa Lacticiniorum* of 1477. Its name probably comes from the mountain peak Fontin.

CULINARY USES

Fontina is delicious eaten on its own, and because it melts beautifully and does not become stringy, it can be used instead of mozzarella in a wide variety of dishes. It is also perfect for making a *fonduta*, the Italian equivalent of a Swiss cheese fondue.

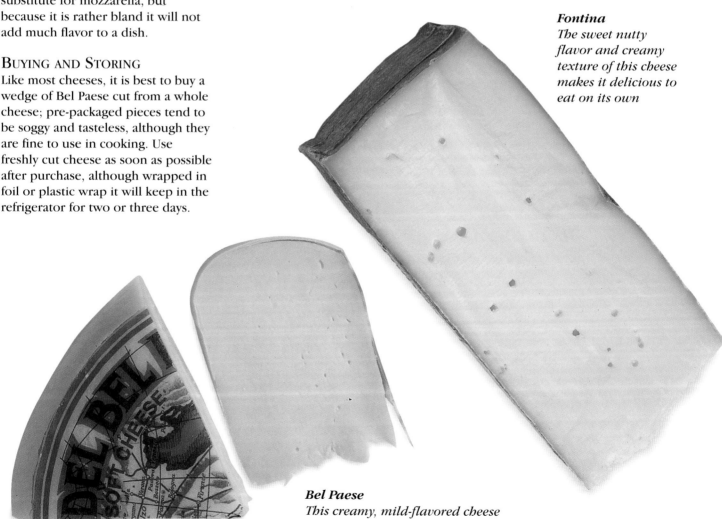

Fontina
The sweet nutty flavor and creamy texture of this cheese makes it delicious to eat on its own

Bel Paese
This creamy, mild-flavored cheese can also be eaten on its own, and it is excellent for cooking, too

Soft Cheeses

Taleggio

A square creamy cheese from Lombardy with a fat content of almost 50 percent, Taleggio has a mild, salty-sweet flavor, which can become pungent if it is left to age for too long (it reaches maturity after only six weeks). The cheeses are dipped in brine for about 14 hours before maturing, which gives them a slightly salty tang. Each cheese with its soft edible rind weighs about 4¼ lb. If you intend to eat the rind, remove the paper from the top.

CULINARY USES

Taleggio is perfect eaten on its own as a cheese course. Like Fontina, it melts into a velvety smoothness when cooked and does not become stringy, so it can be used in any cooked dish that requires a good melting consistency.

BUYING AND STORING

Both Fontina and Taleggio should be eaten as soon as possible after purchase. If necessary, they can be tightly wrapped in waxed paper or plastic wrap and kept in the refrigerator for a day or two.

Stracchino

Stracchino is made from very creamy milk and matured for only about ten days, and never longer than two months. The smooth rindless cheese with a fat content of about 50 percent is reminiscent of Taleggio, but softer-textured and with a sweeter flavor. Robiola is a small, square Stracchino weighing about 3½ oz. Because these cheeses are so delicate, they are wrapped in plasticized paper to preserve their freshness.

HISTORY

The name Stracchino comes from the Lombardian dialect word meaning "tired." It does not reflect on the quality of the cheeses, but merely indicates that they were traditionally made in the winter months when the cows were tired from their long trek down from the mountains to their winter quarters on the plain of Lombardy. Some farmhouse-produced Stracchini are still made only in winter, but most are now produced all year round.

CULINARY USES

Stracchino should only be eaten as a dessert cheese; it is not suitable for cooking. On Christmas Eve in Lombardy, Robiola is served as a special delicacy with the spicy candied fruit relish, *mostarda di Cremona*.

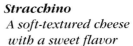

Stracchino
A soft-textured cheese with a sweet flavor

Taleggio
Perfect to eat on its own, Taleggio has a mild, sweet flavor

Robiola
This is a small square stracchino and is always wrapped in paper to preserve its freshness

Soft Cheeses

Gorgonzola

The proper name for this famous blue-veined cheese is Stracchino Gorgonzola, because it is made from the curds of Stracchino. Originally made only in the town of Gorgonzola, the cheese is now produced all over Lombardy.

Gorgonzola is prepared by making alternate layers of hot and cold curds. The difference in temperature causes the layers to separate, leaving air pockets in which the mold (*penicillium glaucum*) will grow. The best Gorgonzola cheeses are left until the mold forms naturally, but more commonly copper wires are inserted into the cheese to encourage the growth. The cheeses are matured from three to five months; the longer the aging, the stronger the flavor.

Gorgonzola is a very creamy cheese, the color of buttermilk, with greenish-blue veining and a fat content of 48 percent. Its flavor can range from very mild (*dolce*) to extremely powerful (*piccante*). The best-known mild version outside Italy is Dolcelatte (sweet milk), which is exceptionally creamy and delicately flavored. Another version, *torta*, consists of Gorgonzola and mascarpone arranged in alternate layers like a cake.

HISTORY

Gorgonzola has been made in the village of the same name since the 1st century AD, when the cheeses were matured in the chilly caves of the Valsassina.

CULINARY USES

Although it is usually eaten as a cheese course, Gorgonzola is also used in cooking, particularly in creamy sauces for vegetables or pasta or as a filling for pancakes and ravioli. It is delicious stirred into soft polenta, or spread on deep-fried polenta *crostini*. Surprisingly, cooking diminishes the flavor of Gorgonzola, so that it does not dominate a delicate dish.

BUYING AND STORING

Supermarkets sell vacuum-packed portions of Gorgonzola, which are acceptable but not nearly as good as a wedge cut from a whole, foil-wrapped cheese. If you don't like a very strong flavor, be sure to buy *gorgonzola dolce* or Dolcelatte. Wrapped in plastic wrap, the cheese will keep for several days in the refrigerator.

Dolcelatte
An exceptionally creamy, delicately flavored Gorgonzola

Torta
This striped cheese consists of layers of Gorgonzola and mascarpone

Gorgonzola
The greenish-blue veining is typical of this classic cheese

Fresh Cheeses

Caprini

These little disc-shaped goat cheeses come from southern Italy. They have a pungent flavor, which becomes even stronger as the cheeses mature. Fresh Caprini do not travel well, so you will rarely find them outside Italy, but they are available bottled in olive oil flavored with herbs and chilies.

CULINARY USES
Fresh goat's cheeses can be fried and served warm with salad leaves as an appetizer, or crumbled over pizzas to make an unusual topping. Bottled Caprini should be drained and eaten as a cheese course. If you like a spicy kick, trickle on some of the oil from the jar, but beware— it will be very piquant.

Caprini
Rarely found fresh outside Italy, these cheeses are usually found bottled in flavored olive oil

Mascarpone

This delicately flavored triple cream cheese from Lombardy is too rich to be eaten on its own (it contains 90 percent fat), but can be used in much the same way as whipped cream and has a similar texture. Mascarpone is made from the cream of curdled cow's milk. It is mildly acidulated and adds a distinctive richness to risottos and creamy pasta sauces. It takes only 24 hours to produce, so it tastes very fresh, with a unique sweetness that makes it ideal for making desserts. A new lighter version called *fiorello light* is now being produced for the health-conscious. While it is useful for those on a diet, it is nothing like the real thing.

CULINARY USES
In Italy, mascarpone is used for savory dishes as well as desserts. It makes wonderfully creamy sauces for pasta and combines well with walnuts and artichokes. Mascarpone can also enhance the texture and flavor of risottos or a white bean soup. It is most commonly used in desserts, either served with fresh berries, or as a filling for pastries. It is an essential ingredient of tiramisù and can be churned into a rich, velvety ice cream.

BUYING AND STORING
Delicatessens in Italy serve fresh mascarpone by the *etto* (about 3½ oz) from large earthenware bowls, but outside Italy it is sold in 9 oz or 1¼ lb plastic tubs. Although the flavor is not as good, pre-packaged cheese will keep for a week in the refrigerator; fresh mascarpone should be eaten immediately.

> ### COOK'S TIP
> *To lighten the texture of mascarpone and make it less rich, fold in some beaten egg white.*

Mascarpone (above and below)
A triple cream cheese that is too rich to eat on its own, but is ideal for dessert; it is an essential ingredient in tiramisù

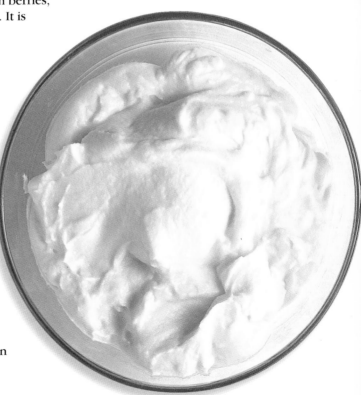

Fresh Cheeses

Cow's milk mozzarella
Known as fior di latte—*"flower of the milk"*

Mozzarella
The best is made from buffalo milk

Smoked mozzarella
This cheese has a very smooth texture, a rich golden color and an interesting smoky flavor

Mozzarella

Italian cooking could hardly exist without mozzarella, the pure white, egg-shaped fresh cheese whose melting quality makes it perfect for so many dishes. The best mozzarella is made in the area around Naples, using water buffalo's milk. It has a moist, springy texture and a deliciously milky flavor. The cheeses are made by the *pasta filata* (layering) method, where the curds are cut into strips, then covered with boiling water. As they rise to the surface, they are torn into shreds and scrunched into egg-shaped balls each weighing about 7 oz. These are placed in light brine for 12 hours, then packed in their own whey inside a paper or plastic wrapping to keep them fresh.

Other types of mozzarella include a cow's milk version called *fior di latte* (flower of the milk) and tiny balls of cheese called *bocconcini* (little mouthfuls). Sometimes, the cheese is wound into braids called *trecce*. All these are fresh cheeses, but mozzarella can also be smoked, which gives it a golden-brown color and an interesting flavor. You will also find in supermarkets a pale yellow semi-hard mozzarella, which is sometimes sold ready-grated. This is the type used in cheap pizzas; it resembles mozzarella only in name and should be avoided.

HISTORY

No one is quite sure when water buffaloes were brought to Italy from India. They may have been introduced by the Greeks or the early Christians; certainly by the sixteenth century they had become a feature of southern Italian agricultural life. At this time, farmers began to use the buffalo milk to make mozzarella. Its popularity soon spread to the northern regions, where cheese-makers started to produce inferior versions made from cow's milk.

CULINARY USES

Fresh mozzarella is delicious served in an *insalata tricolore*, a salad in the colors of Italy, with white mozzarella, red tomatoes and fresh green basil. Smoked mozzarella is good in sandwiches or as part of an *antipasto*. When cooked, mozzarella becomes uniquely stringy, so it is perfect for topping pizzas or filling *mozzarella in carrozza* (mozzarella in a carriage), sandwiches dipped in beaten egg and deep-fried. A favorite Roman dish is *supplì al telefono*: mozzarella wrapped inside balls of cooked rice and fried until it melts to resemble telephone wires.

BUYING AND STORING

Cow's milk mozzarella is perfectly adequate for cooking, but for a really fine cheese buy *mozzarella di bufala*. Unopened, mozzarella will keep in the refrigerator for several days, but once the wrapping has been pierced it should be eaten as soon as possible. Opened mozzarella can be kept for a brief time in a covered bowl containing the whey from the bag or, failing that, skim milk or lightly salted water.

Mozzarella bocconcini
The name means "little mouthfuls"

Ricotta
Widely used in
Italian cooking,
ricotta can be
combined with
spinach for a ravioli
filling, or used in
desserts, such as
cheesecake

Ricotta salata
This hard, salted version of the
cheese has a compact, flaky texture
and can be used as a substitute for
Parmesan or Pecorino

Ricotta

Ricotta derives its name (literally "recooked") from the process of reheating the leftover whey from hard cheeses and adding a little fresh milk to make a soft white curd cheese with a rather solid yet granular consistency and a fat content of only about 20 percent. The freshly made cheeses are traditionally put into baskets to drain and take their hemispherical shape and markings from these *cestelli* (little baskets).

Commercially produced ricotta is made from cow's milk, but in rural areas sheep's or goat's milk is sometimes used.

Ricotta salata is a hard, salted version of the cheese, made from the whey of Pecorino. It has a compact, flaky texture and looks rather like a hard Pecorino.

CULINARY USES

Ricotta is widely used in Italian cooking for both savory and sweet dishes. It has an excellent texture but very little intrinsic flavor, so it makes a perfect vehicle for seasonings such as black pepper and nutmeg or chopped fresh herbs. In its best-known form, it is puréed with cooked spinach to make a classic filling for ravioli, cannelloni or lasagne, or delicious light gnocchi.

It is often used in desserts, such as baked cheesecakes, or it can be sweetened and served with fruit.

Hard *ricotta salata* can be grated and used as a lower-fat substitute for Parmesan or Pecorino.

BUYING AND STORING

Fresh ricotta should always be eaten the day it is bought, as it quickly develops a sour taste. Most supermarkets sell a pre-packaged version of the cheese, which stays fresh longer.

Ricotta salata is sometimes sold in pre-packaged wedges, but for a good flavor and texture you should buy it freshly cut from a whole cheese. Tightly wrapped in foil, it will keep in the refrigerator for up to a month.

Cured Meats & Sausages

Every region of Italy has its own special cured meats and sausages, each differing as widely as the regions themselves. Prosciutto crudo *and* salame *appear in every guise and often constitute an* antipasto (appetizer) *on their own.*

HISTORY

Italy was traditionally an agricultural country, so almost every rural family kept a pig and cured every part of it, from snout to tail, to provide food for the family throughout the year. In any Italian larder, a range of home-cured hams, sausages and bacon would be found hanging from the ceiling. Nowadays hundreds of different types of hams, cured meats and sausages are commercially produced, many still using the old artisanal methods. Wherever you travel in Italy, you will find regional variations on the same theme.

Most of these cured meats are served as an *antipasto* before a meal. A Tuscan *antipasto* will consist of a selection of thinly sliced *affettati* (sliced ham and *salame*), and it is sometimes served with pickled vegetables, which are designed to whet the appetite.

Prosciutto

Italy is famous for its *prosciutto crudo*, salted and air-dried ham that requires no cooking. The most famous of these hams, *prosciutto di Parma*, comes from the area around Parma, where Parmesan cheese is also made. The pigs in this region are fed partly on the whey from the cheese-making process, which makes their flesh very mild and sweet. Because they are always reared and kept in sheds and never allowed to roam outdoors, they tend to be rather fatty. Parma hams are made from the pig's hindquarters, which are lightly salted and air-dried for at least one year (and sometimes up to two). The zone of production of Parma ham is restricted by law to the area between the Taro and Baganza rivers, where the air and humidity levels are ideal for drying and curing the hams. In fact, every year thousands of ready-salted hams are sent here from neighboring regions to be dried and cured in the unique air around Parma.

Prosciutto di Parma
The most famous Italian ham comes from the area around Parma, where Parmesan is also made

Prosciutto cotto

Italy also produces a range of cooked hams, usually boiled. They can be flavored with all sorts of herbs and spices. Cooked ham is sometimes served as an *antipasto* together with raw ham, but it is more often eaten in sandwiches and snacks.

San Daniele

Some people regard these hams from the Friuli region as superior even to Parma ham. San Daniele pigs are kept outside, so their flesh is leaner, and their diet of acorns gives it a distinctive flavor. San Daniele is produced in much smaller quantities than Parma ham, which makes it even more expensive.

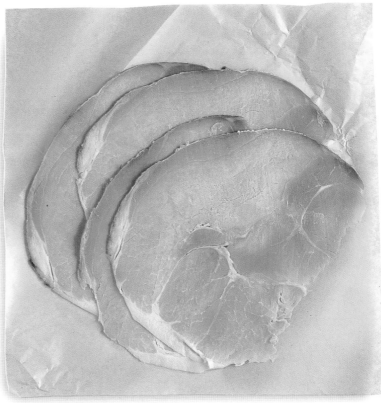

Prosciutto cotto
This cooked ham is sometimes served with sliced cured hams as an antipasto

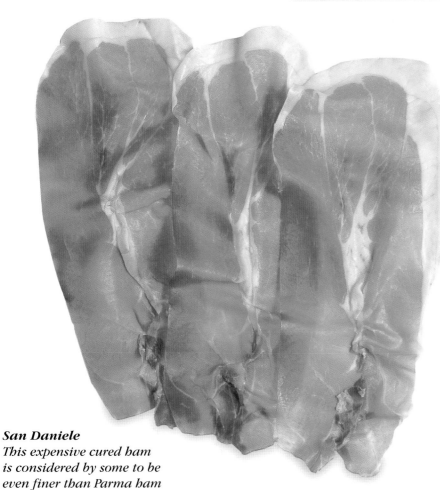

San Daniele
This expensive cured ham is considered by some to be even finer than Parma ham

CULINARY USES
Wafer-thin slices of *prosciutto crudo* are delicious served with melon or fresh figs or, when these are out of season, with little cubes of unsalted butter. If you serve bread with this ham, that too should be unsalted to counterbalance the salty-sweetness of the ham. *Prosciutto crudo* can be rolled up with thin slices of veal and sage leaves and pan-fried in butter and white wine or Marsala to make *saltimbocca alla romana*, finely chopped and added to risotti and pasta sauces, or used as a filling for ravioli.

BUYING AND STORING
The best part of the ham comes from the center. Avoid buying the end pieces, which are very salty and rather chewy. Because *prosciutto crudo* should be very thinly sliced, buy only what you need at any one time or it may dry out. Ideally you should eat it on the day it is bought, although it will keep in the refrigerator for up to three days.

Cured Meats

Pancetta and Lardo

Pancetta resembles unsmoked bacon, except that it is not sold sliced, but rolled up into a sausage shape. It is made from pork belly, which is cured in salt and spices to give it a mild flavor. *Lardo* is very similar (but flat) and less readily available.

CULINARY USES

Pancetta can be eaten raw as an *antipasto* (although it is very fatty), but it is usually cut into strips and cooked like bacon. It is an essential ingredient for *spaghetti alla carbonara*.

Pancetta

These round rolled slices of cured pork belly are the Italian equivalent of unsmoked bacon

Smoked pancetta

The smoked version of pancetta *is sold in thin strips rather than being rolled*

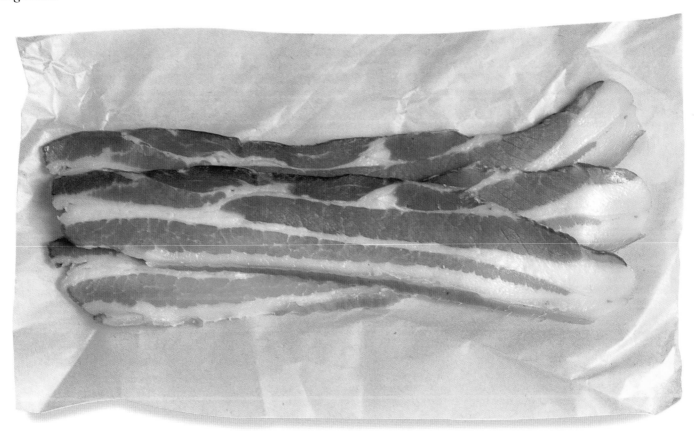

Speck

This fatty bacon is made from pork belly, which is smoke-cured over beechwood with herbs and spices, then air-dried. Sometimes it is covered with peppercorns or dried herbs, which add a distinctive flavor. It comes from the Tyrol, near the Swiss border, which explains its German-sounding name.

Culinary Uses

Speck is too fatty to be eaten raw, but it is used to add flavor to soups, stews and sauces. It is excellent cooked with fresh peas or lentils.

Buying and Storing

Italian bacon is sold by sections, not sliced. Wrapped in plastic wrap, *pancetta*, *lardo* and *speck* will keep in the refrigerator for up to one month.

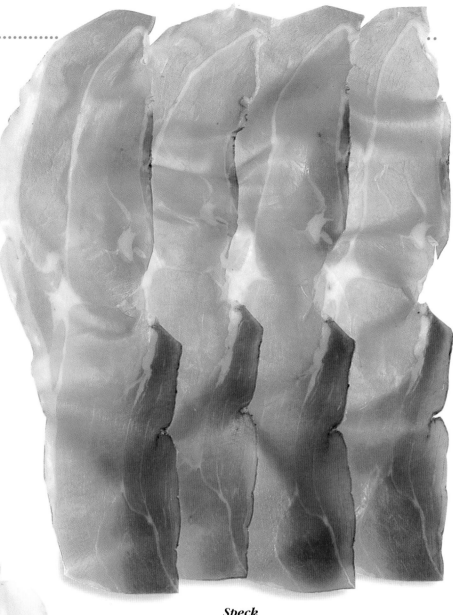

Speck
A fatty ham, smoke-cured over beechwood with herbs and spices, then air-dried

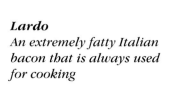

Lardo
An extremely fatty Italian bacon that is always used for cooking

Cured Meats

Bresaola

This cured raw beef is a specialty of Valtellina in Lombardy, but it is eaten and enjoyed all over Italy. It can be made from any cut of beef, but prime fillet produces the best bresaola. It is first cured in salt, then air-dried for many months before being pressed to produce an intensely dark red meat, which resembles *prosciutto crudo* in flavor, but is more delicate and less salty. Like *prosciutto crudo*, it is always sliced wafer-thin and served in small quantities, so you don't need to buy very much. Each bresaola weighs 4¼–6¼ lb, depending on the size of the original cut of beef.

CULINARY USES

Bresaola is often served as an *antipasto*, sliced very thinly and simply dressed with a drizzle of extra virgin olive oil and a sprinkling of fresh lemon juice. In Lombardy, bresaola is sometimes wrapped around a filling of soft goat cheese and then rolled up like cannelloni.

BUYING AND STORING

Only buy bresaola made from beef fillet. You can tell the type from the shape; that made from fillet is long with rounded edges, like the original cut of beef, while the cheaper bresaola made from other leg cuts is pressed into an oblong shape. Use it as soon as possible after slicing, preferably the same day, or it will dry out and develop an unpleasantly sharp flavor.

Bresaola
The delicate flavor of this salt-cured beef makes it perfect to serve, thinly sliced, as an antipasto

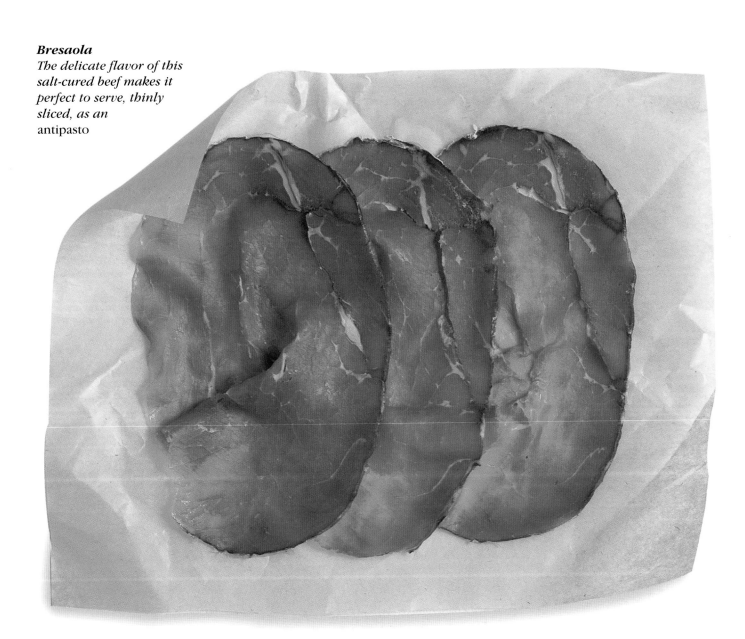

Sausages

Coppa

This salted and dried sausage is made from neck or shoulder of pork, and the casing is made from natural skin. *Coppa* has a roughly rectangular shape and a rich deep red color. It comes from Lombardy and Emilia Romagna, although, confusingly, in Rome you will find a *coppa* that is a sort of pig's head brawn (this variety is never exported).

Zampone

This speciality sausage from Modena is a pig's leg stuffed with minced pork shoulder and other cuts, including some skin. The stuffing has a creamy texture and the skin of the leg encloses it to retain its original shape, complete with feet. Each zampone weighs up to 4¼ lb.

Coppa
Roughly rectangular in shape, this sausage has a rich, deep red color

Zampone
A partially-cooked zampone needs only to be heated through

COOKING ZAMPONE

A raw zampone needs to be boiled for 2–3 hours, depending on the size, although some vacuum-packed varieties are already partially-cooked and need only to be heated through. For a fresh zampone, make a couple of slits in the skin and cook in the same way as cotechino. Zampone is traditionally sliced into rings and served with lentils or mashed potatoes. A bollito misto often contains a zampone.

Sausages

Italy boasts almost as many different sausages as there are towns. Practically all are made with pork, although venison and wild boar sausages are popular in country areas. Most sausages and salami are factory-produced today, but many towns in Italy still have *salumerie* (sausage shops) selling homemade sausages flavored with local produce, such as wild mushrooms or herbs and spices. The most famous sausage-producing town is Bologna. Fresh sausages are made from coarsely chopped pork and contain a high proportion of fat for extra flavor. They are usually sold in links, tied together with string. Most Italian sausages, however, are cured and ready to eat.

Luganega

A specialty of northern Italy, luganega is a mild, spiced country sausage made from pork, which often contains Parmesan cheese. Sometimes known as *salsiccia a metro*, because it is sold in a long continuous rope, coiled up like a snake, and is sold by the foot or whatever length you require. It can be grilled or pan-fried with white wine and is often served on a bed of lentils or mashed potatoes. Luganega can also be cut into short lengths and stirred into a hearty risotto.

Cotechino

A large fresh pork sausage weighing about 2¼ lb, which has been lightly spiced and salted for only a few days. Cotechino is a specialty of Emilia Romagna, Lombardy and the Veneto. It takes its name from *coteca,* meaning "skin."

COOKING COTECHINO

Cotechino is boiled and served hot, often as part of a bollito misto *(mixed boiled meats). Pierce the skin in several places and place the sausage in a large saucepan. Cover with cold water and bring slowly to a boil, then simmer slowly for 2–3 hours.*

Slice the cotechino thickly and serve on a bed of cooked lentils, mashed potatoes or cannellini beans.

Luganega
This mildly spiced sausage, which is coiled up like a snake, is sold by the foot, or whatever length you require

Speck

This fatty bacon is made from pork belly, which is smoke-cured over beechwood with herbs and spices, then air-dried. Sometimes it is covered with peppercorns or dried herbs, which add a distinctive flavor. It comes from the Tyrol, near the Swiss border, which explains its German-sounding name.

CULINARY USES

Speck is too fatty to be eaten raw, but it is used to add flavor to soups, stews and sauces. It is excellent cooked with fresh peas or lentils.

BUYING AND STORING

Italian bacon is sold by sections, not sliced. Wrapped in plastic wrap, *pancetta*, *lardo* and *speck* will keep in the refrigerator for up to one month.

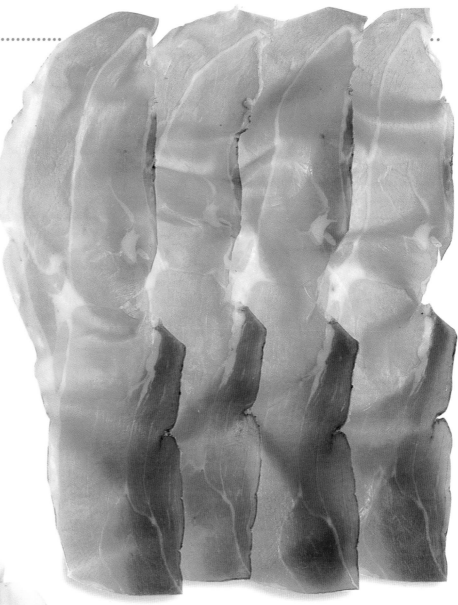

Speck
A fatty ham, smoke-cured over beechwood with herbs and spices, then air-dried

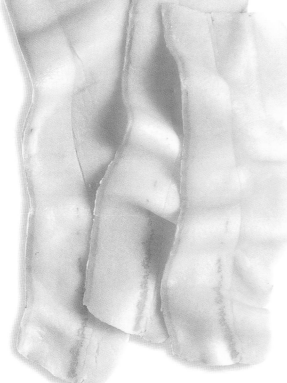

Lardo
An extremely fatty Italian bacon that is always used for cooking

Cured Meats

Bresaola

This cured raw beef is a specialty of Valtellina in Lombardy, but it is eaten and enjoyed all over Italy. It can be made from any cut of beef, but prime fillet produces the best bresaola. It is first cured in salt, then air-dried for many months before being pressed to produce an intensely dark red meat, which resembles *prosciutto crudo* in flavor, but is more delicate and less salty. Like *prosciutto crudo*, it is always sliced wafer-thin and served in small

quantities, so you don't need to buy very much. Each bresaola weighs 4¼–6¼ lb, depending on the size of the original cut of beef.

CULINARY USES

Bresaola is often served as an *antipasto*, sliced very thinly and simply dressed with a drizzle of extra virgin olive oil and a sprinkling of fresh lemon juice. In Lombardy, bresaola is sometimes wrapped around a filling of soft goat cheese and then rolled up like cannelloni.

BUYING AND STORING

Only buy bresaola made from beef fillet. You can tell the type from the shape; that made from fillet is long with rounded edges, like the original cut of beef, while the cheaper bresaola made from other leg cuts is pressed into an oblong shape. Use it as soon as possible after slicing, preferably the same day, or it will dry out and develop an unpleasantly sharp flavor.

Bresaola
The delicate flavor of this salt-cured beef makes it perfect to serve, thinly sliced, as an antipasto

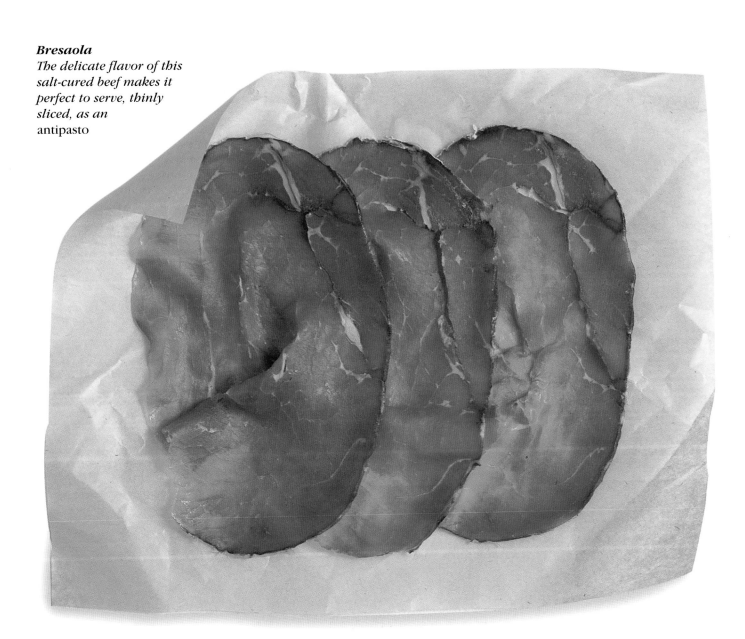

Mortadella

The most famous of all the sausages from Bologna, mortadella is also the largest, often having a diameter of up to 18 in. Today it is cooked in hot-air ovens to a core temperature of 140°F, which means that it will keep for several weeks. It is considered to be the finest Italian pork sausage, with its wonderfully smooth texture, although it has a rather bland flavor. Apart from its huge size, mortadella is distinctive for its delicate, pale pink color studded with cubes of creamy white fat and sometimes pale green pistachios. It is the original bologna.

BUYING

Authentic Bolognese mortadella is made only from pure pork, but cheaper varieties may contain all sorts of other ingredients, such as beef, tripe, pig's head, soy flour and artificial colorings.

Beware of mortadella that looks too violently pink and, if you are buying it sliced and pre-packaged, check the ingredients on the package before you buy.

CULINARY USES

Mortadella is usually thinly sliced and eaten cold, either in a sandwich or as part of a plate of assorted cold meats as an *antipasto*. It can also be cubed and stirred into risotto or pasta sauces just before the end of cooking, or finely chopped to make an excellent stuffing for poultry or filled pasta.

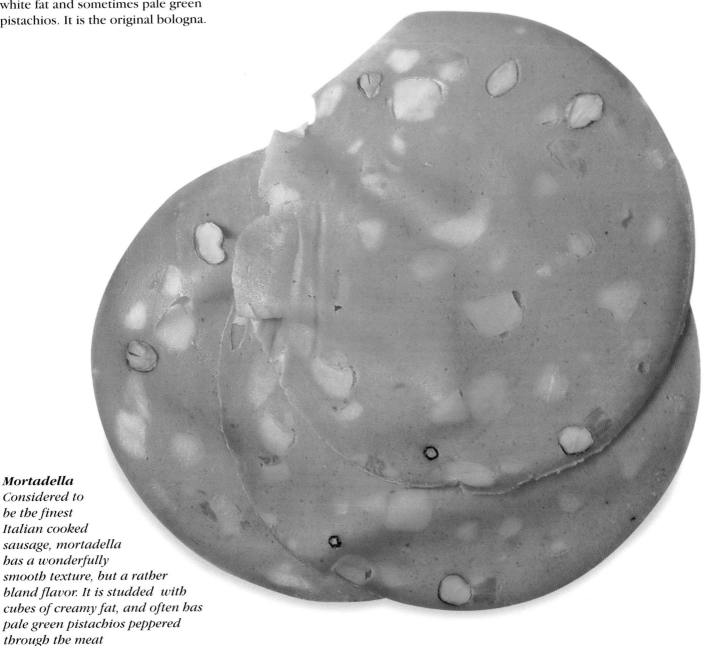

Mortadella
Considered to be the finest Italian cooked sausage, mortadella has a wonderfully smooth texture, but a rather bland flavor. It is studded with cubes of creamy fat, and often has pale green pistachios peppered through the meat

Salame

Salame

There are dozens of types of *salame*, whose texture and flavor reflect the character and traditions of the different regions of Italy. Essentially, all *salami* are made from pure pork, but the finished product varies according to the kind of meat used, the proportion of lean meat to fat, how finely it is minced, the seasonings and the period of drying and seasoning.

Salame di Felino

This soft, coarse-cut sausage comes from Felino near Parma and is regarded as one of the finest Italian *salami*. It has a very high proportion of lean pork to fat

and is flavored with peppercorns, a small amount of garlic and the local white wine. Because it is only very lightly cured, it has a very delicate flavor but does not keep well. You may find it at good Italian delicatessens, where it is easily recognizable by its uneven truncheon shape, which makes it look handmade. Like its neighbor, Parma ham, *salame di Felino* is very expensive, but well worth the cost.

Salame fiorentino

This large, coarse-cut pork sausage from Tuscany is often flavored with fennel seeds and pepper, when it is known as *finocchiona*. The fennel gives it a very distinctive flavor.

Salame di Felino
One of the finest Italian salami—*this lightly cured sausage is flavored with peppercorns, garlic and white wine*

Salame fiorentino
This coarse-cut pork sausage from Tuscany is often flavored with fennel seeds and pepper

Salame milano

Probably the most commonly found of all *salami*, this Milanese sausage is made from equal quantities of finely minced pork, fat and beef, seasoned with pepper, garlic and white wine. It is deep red in color and speckled with grains of fat resembling rice. Also known as *crespone*, it is mass-produced and regarded as inferior to most other *salami*. There is also a small whole *salame milanese*, weighing about 1¼ lb, called *cacciatoro*, which is cured and matured for a much shorter time and has a more delicate flavor and softer texture.

Salame sardo

This fiery red *salame* from Sardinia is a rustic sausage flavored with red pepper. A similar sausage is *salame napoletano* from Naples, which uses a mixture of black and red pepper for a powerful kick.

Salame ungherese

Despite its name, this *salame* is manufactured in Italy, using a Hungarian recipe. It is made from very finely minced pure pork or pork and beef, and flavored with paprika, pepper, garlic and white wine. The fat is evenly spread throughout the sausage, giving it a mottled appearance.

BUYING AND STORING
With the exception of *salame di Felino*, almost all *salami* can be bought ready-sliced and vacuum-packed, but taste much better if they are freshly cut from a whole *salame*. A good delicatessen will slice the *salame* to the thickness you require.

Salame ungherese
Made in Italy from a Hungarian recipe

Salame sardo
A fiery salame *flavored with red pepper*

Salame napoletano
Similar to salame sardo, *this salame uses a mix of black and red pepper*

Salame milano

Cacciatoro
This small whole salame milanese *is cured and matured for only a short time*

Meat & Poultry

Until recently, meat did not figure largely in Italian cooking, which relied much more heavily on the peasant staples of pasta, bread, vegetables and, in coastal areas, fish. As the country became more prosperous, however, more people added meat to their daily diet, and now animals are farmed all over Italy to provide veal, pork, beef, lamb and goat.

Veal is a favorite meat in Italy and appears in innumerable recipes from every region. The best comes from milk-fed calves that are reared in Piedmont. The area around Rome is famous for its lamb, and spit-roasted suckling lamb and goat are popular specialties of the region. Superb beef cattle are bred in Tuscany, but the beef from other regions comes from working cattle that have reached the end of their useful lives, and is best used for stews and dishes that require long, slow cooking.

Many peasant families in Italy still own a pig, which provides pork as well as a huge variety of hams, sausages and other cured meats. Every part of the pig is eaten in one form or another, from snout to tail. Indeed, Italians never waste any edible part of their meat, so offal of all kinds is used in many dishes. A Tuscan *fritto misto* is composed of a variety of offal ranging from brains to sweetbreads and lungs, while the Milanese version also includes cockscombs—so, unless you are an offal lover, be warned if you see these dishes on a menu!

Poultry is another popular food. Factory farming does exist in Italy, but many flavorful free-range birds are still available. Chicken, guinea fowl and turkey appear in a huge variety of simple and delicious dishes and are usually filleted for quick cooking. Duck and goose make their appearance, too, often cooked with sharp fruits to counteract the richness of the meat. Many recipes use wild duck, shot by the enthusiastic (some say over-enthusiastic) hunters who abound in every region. Mercifully, the Italian habit of shooting every type of wild bird,

whether edible or not, is less prevalent than it was, but hunters are lax about observing a close season for shooting, so game, both feathered and furred, seems to be available almost all year round.

Abbacchio and agnello (lamb)

Lambs are bred mainly in southern Italy, particularly in the area around Rome. They are slaughtered at different ages, resulting in distinctive flavors and textures. The youngest lamb is *abbacchio*, month-old milk-fed lamb from Lazio, whose pale pinkish flesh is meltingly tender. *Abbacchio* is usually spit-roasted whole. Spring lamb, about four months old, is often sold as *abbacchio*. It has darker flesh, which is also very tender and can be used for roasting or grilling. A leg of spring lamb weighs about 2¼–3½ lb. Older lamb (*agnello*) has a slightly stronger flavor and is suitable for roasting or stewing.

Lamb cutlets
Allow at least three small, succulent lamb cutlets like these per serving.

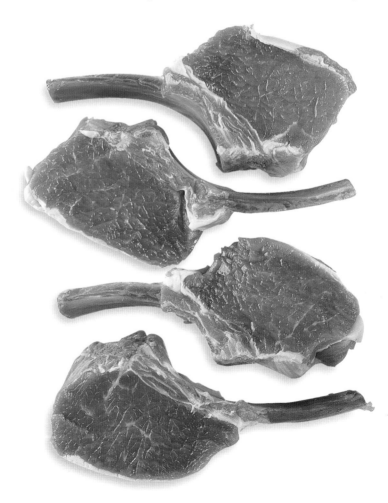

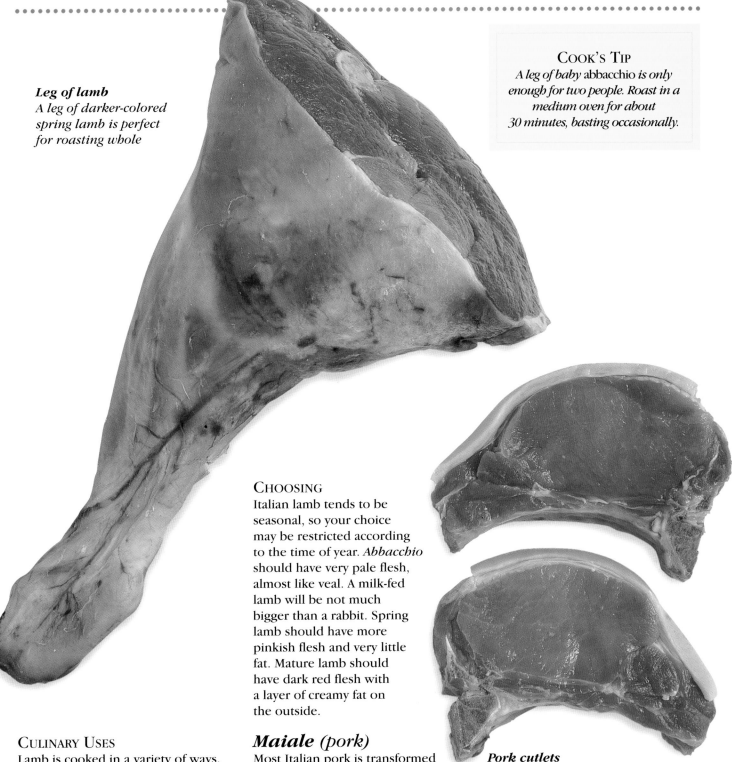

Leg of lamb
A leg of darker-colored spring lamb is perfect for roasting whole

CHOOSING

Italian lamb tends to be seasonal, so your choice may be restricted according to the time of year. *Abbacchio* should have very pale flesh, almost like veal. A milk-fed lamb will be not much bigger than a rabbit. Spring lamb should have more pinkish flesh and very little fat. Mature lamb should have dark red flesh with a layer of creamy fat on the outside.

CULINARY USES

Lamb is cooked in a variety of ways, from *al forno* (roast) to *costolette alla milanese* (fried breaded cutlets). Roast lamb is the traditional Easter dish. It is not cut into thin slices, but served in large chunks, which should be so tender that they fall off the bone. A favorite recipe for spring lamb is *agnello alla giudea* (Jewish-style lamb), braised in a delicate egg and lemon sauce.

Maiale (pork)

Most Italian pork is transformed into sausages, *salami* and hams, but fresh meat is enjoyed all over Italy, often combined with local herbs such as rosemary, fennel or sage. Different regions eat different parts of the pig; Tuscany is famous for its *arista di maiale alla fiorentina*, (loin of pork roasted with rosemary), while in Naples *il musso* (the snout) is considered a great delicacy.

Pork cutlets
Tender chops or cutlets can be grilled or braised with herbs

CULINARY USES

Pork chops or cutlets can be grilled or braised with herbs or artichokes. Loin of pork is deliciously tender braised in milk (*arrosto di maiale al latte*), or it can be roasted with rosemary or sage.

Meat & Poultry

Manzo (beef)

Italian beef has an unjustifiably poor reputation. It is true that in agricultural areas, particularly the south, beef can be stringy and tough. This is because the cattle are working animals, not bred for the table, and are only eaten toward the end of their hard-working life. This type of beef is only suitable for long, slow-cooked country stews. In Tuscany, however, superb beef cattle from Val di Chiana produce meat that can rival any other world-renowned beef and provide the magnificent *bistecche alla fiorentina* (T-bone steaks).

CULINARY USES

Thick-cut T-bone steaks (*bistecche alla fiorentina*) from Val di Chiana cattle are grilled over wood fires until well-browned on the outside and very rare inside. Rump or fillet steaks are also cooked very rare and sliced on the bias as a *tagliata*. A modern creation is *carpaccio*, wafer-thin slices of raw beef marinated in olive oil and herbs and served as an *antipasto*. Thinly sliced topside is rolled around a stuffing to make *involtini* (beef olives). A favorite Italian family dish is *bollito misto*, a mixture of boiled meats and offal including beef. Leftover boiled beef can be sliced and made into a salad.

Less tender cuts of meat are usually braised, stewed or ground to be used in *ragù* (meat sauce) or *polpettone* (meat loaf).

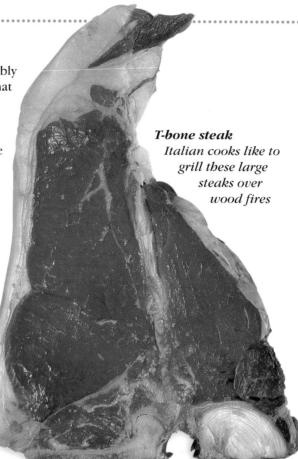

T-bone steak
Italian cooks like to grill these large steaks over wood fires

Beef olives
Thinly sliced topside rolled around a flavorful stuffing

Minced beef
Less tender cuts of beef are ground and used for ragù *(meat sauce) or* polpettone *(meat loaf)*

Carpaccio
These wafer-thin slices of raw beef are simply marinated in olive oil and served as an antipasto

Frattaglie (offal)

Nothing is wasted by Italian butchers, so a huge variety of offal is available. Liver is a great favorite; the finest is *fegato di vitello*, tender calf's liver, which is regarded as a luxury. Chicken livers are popular for topping *crostini* or for pasta sauces, and pork liver is a specialty of Tuscany. Butchers often sell pig's liver ready-wrapped in natural caul (*rete*), which keeps the liver tender as it cooks. Lamb's and calf's kidneys (*rognoni* or *rognoncini*), brains (*cervello*) and sweetbreads (*animelle*) are specialties of northern Italy. The latter two are similar in texture and flavor, but sweetbreads are creamier and more delicate. Every region has its own recipes for tripe (*trippa*); this almost always comes from veal calves rather than other cattle, whose tripe has a coarser texture and flavor. All parts of a veal calf are considered great delicacies. The head is used in *bollito misto* (mixed boiled meats), and the legs give substance to soups and stews. Oxtail (*coda di bue*) comes from older beef cattle.

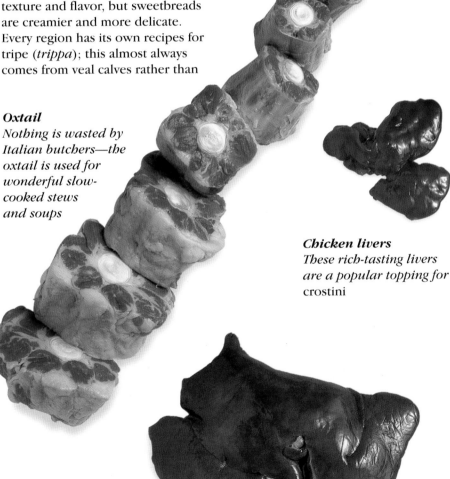

Oxtail
Nothing is wasted by Italian butchers—the oxtail is used for wonderful slow-cooked stews and soups

Chicken livers
These rich-tasting livers are a popular topping for crostini

Pig's liver
This is a specialty of Tuscany

Calf's liver
Thinly sliced, this is often simply pan-fried with onions

COOKING OFFAL

Most offal will benefit from being soaked in milk before cooking to remove any coarseness of flavor. Some types, such as liver and brains, require very little cooking in order to preserve their delicate texture. In Venice, thinly sliced calf's liver is cooked with onions to make *fegato alla veneziana*; this is often served with grilled polenta. The Milanese version is coated in egg and bread crumbs and fried in butter. The simplest and one of the most delicious ways with liver is to sauté it quickly in butter with fresh sage. Brains and sweetbreads can be blanched, then quickly fried in butter, or pounded to a paste and made into croquettes (*crocchette*). Kidneys should be sautéed in butter, or braised with wine and onions or Marsala (*trifolati*). Pre-prepared (dressed) tripe will have been scrubbed, soaked and boiled by the butcher, but it should still be blanched for 30 minutes before cooking. Tripe can be prepared *alla fiorentina* in tomato sauce flavored with oregano or marjoram; the version from Parma (*alla parmigiana*) is fried in butter and topped with Parmesan cheese, while in Bologna, eggs are added to the mixture.

Meat & Poultry

Vitello (veal)

Veal is the most popular meat in Italy and appears in hundreds of different recipes. Like lamb, calves are slaughtered at different ages to produce different qualities of meat. The best and most expensive veal is *vitello di latte* from Piedmont and Lombardy. The calves are fed only on milk and are slaughtered at just a few weeks old, producing extremely tender, very pale meat with no fat. Older calves, up to nine months old, are known as *vitello*. Their flesh is still tender, but darker in color than milk-fed veal. *Vitellone* is somewhere between veal and beef. It comes from bullocks aged between one and three years, who have never worked in the fields and whose flesh is therefore still quite tender and lighter in color than beef.

CULINARY USES

Young, milk-fed veal is ideal for *scaloppine* (scallops) and *piccate* (thin scallops), which need very little cooking. *Vitello* can be served as chops, cutlets or a rolled roast. The shin is cut into *osso buco* (literally "bone with a hole"), complete with bone marrow, or *stinco* (the whole shin), and braised until meltingly tender. An unusual combination that works wonderfully well is *vitello tonnato*, cold roast veal thinly sliced and coated in a rich tuna sauce. *Vitellone* should be treated like tender beef. It can be grilled, roasted or casseroled, but it is not suitable for scallops or similar cuts.

CHOOSING

Young veal should have very pale, slightly rosy fine-grained flesh with no trace of fat. *Vitellone* should be pinker and paler than beef, with only a faint marbling of fat, and should feel firm, not flabby. Scallops and *piccate* must be cut only from very young veal. They should be sliced across the grain so that they keep their shape and do not shrivel during cooking. If you are buying boned veal, ask the butcher to give you the bones, which make wonderful stock.

Veal scallops
These are always sliced very thinly across the grain

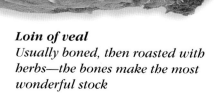

Loin of veal
Usually boned, then roasted with herbs—the bones make the most wonderful stock

Cinghiale (wild boar)

Wild boar are the ancestors of domestic pigs, which used to roam in large numbers in the forests of Tuscany and Sardinia, but which are becoming increasingly rare because of widespread hunting. Baby wild boar are an enchanting sight, with light brown fur striped with horizontal black bands. The adults have coarse, brown coats and fierce-looking tusks. The flesh of a young *cinghiale* is as pale and tender as pork; older animals have very dark flesh, which is tougher but full of flavor.

CULINARY USES

Haunches of wild boar are made into hams, which are displayed in butchers' shops. Young animals can be cooked in the same way as pork. Older boar must be marinated for at least 24 hours to tenderize the meat before roasting or casseroling. The classic sweet and sour sauce, (*agrodolce*), sharpened with red wine vinegar, complements the gamey flavor of the meat.

Coniglio (rabbit) and lepre (hare)

Farmed and wild rabbits often replace chicken or veal in Italian cooking. The meat is very pale and lean and the taste is somewhere between that of good-quality farmhouse chicken and veal. Wild rabbit has a stronger flavor, which combines well with robust flavors; farmed rabbit is very tender and much more delicate.

Hare cannot be farmed, so the only animals available come from the wild. Despite the popularity of hunting in Italy, the hare population has not been totally decimated. The wily creatures, who mange to escape the gun, continue to breed. A hare weighs about twice as much as a rabbit (4¼ lb is about average). The flesh is a rich, dark brown and has a strong gamey flavor similar to that of wild rabbit.

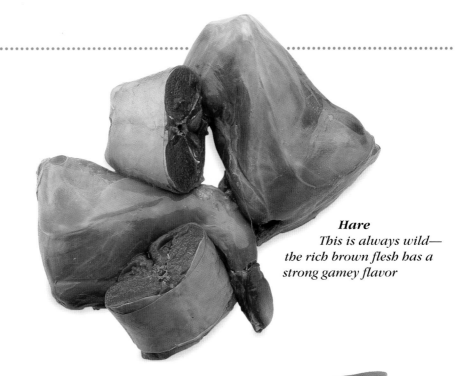

Hare
This is always wild—the rich brown flesh has a strong gamey flavor

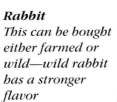

Rabbit
This can be bought either farmed or wild—wild rabbit has a stronger flavor

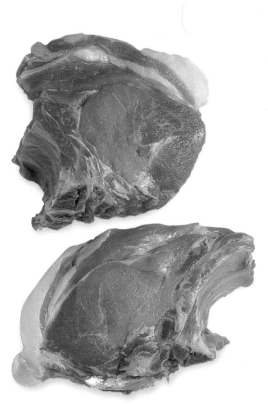

Wild boar
Chops like these can be cooked in the same way as pork

Culinary Uses

Farmed rabbit can replace chicken or turkey in almost any recipe. Wild rabbit can be stewed or braised in white wine or Marsala, or with eggplants, bacon and tomatoes. It can be roasted with root vegetables or fresh herbs. In Sicily, rabbit is often cooked with raisins and pine nuts in an *agrodolce* (sweet and sour) sauce.

Hare is generally casseroled in red wine or Marsala, cooked *in agrodolce* or made into a rich sauce for pappardelle or other wide noodles. Both rabbit and hare are often served with polenta or fried bread.

Cooking Rabbit and Hare

Wild rabbit and hare must be cut into six or eight pieces and marinated in red wine and herbs for 24 hours before cooking. If you like a sweet and sour flavor (game in agrodolce is very popular in Italy), add plenty of red wine vinegar to the marinade. A rabbit weighing about 2¼ lb when cleaned will need about 1½ hour's braising or stewing; a hare needs about 2 hours.

Meat & Poultry

Fagiano (pheasant)

Occasionally, in the Italian countryside, you may still catch a glimpse of a pheasant with its beautiful plumage and long tail feathers. Cock pheasants have bright, iridescent blue and green feathers, while hens are browner and less dramatic-looking. Pheasant farming is still unknown in Italy, and wild pheasants are something of a rarity, so they are regarded as a luxury. They are not hung, but are eaten almost as soon as they are shot, so their flavor is less gamey than in some other countries. Although pheasants are expensive, they are meaty birds for their size, so a cock pheasant will feed three to four people and a hen pheasant two to three.

CULINARY USES

Hen pheasants are smaller than cocks, but their meat is juicier and the flavor is finer. Young hen pheasants can be roasted with or without a stuffing, but cock birds are more suitable for casseroling. Pheasant breast can tend to be dry, so it should be well wrapped with bacon or thickly smeared with butter before roasting. A big pat of butter placed inside the cavity will help to keep the flesh moist. For special occasions, pheasants can be stuffed with candied fruits or pomegranate seeds and nuts. Pheasant breasts can be sautéed and served with a wine or balsamic vinegar sauce, but they can sometimes be rather dry.

Pheasant
Usually eaten as soon as they are shot, Italian pheasants are less gamey than in some other countries. Remember that pheasants contain lead-shot pellets, so take care not to bite down on these!

COOKING PHEASANTS

Unless you know for sure that a pheasant is very young, it is best to wrap the breast in fatty bacon before roasting to prevent dryness. To roast a pheasant, put a pat of butter inside the cavity, or make a stuffing, drape bacon rashers over the breast and roast at 400 °F for about 40 minutes, until tender. Plain roast pheasant is often served with a risotto. Pheasant can also be pot-roasted or casseroled with wine and herbs. If you are serving cock birds, it is worth removing the lower part of the legs after cooking, as they contain hard sinews that are not pleasant to eat.

COOKING QUAIL

Quail should be browned in butter until golden all over, then roasted in a hot oven for about 15 minutes. Their flavor is well complemented by the fruit of the vine, so they are often served with a light sauce containing grapes or raisins soaked in grappa. They can also be wrapped in vine leaves before roasting, which keeps them moist and adds a delicious flavor.

Quaglie (quail)

These small migratory birds are found in Italy throughout the summer months. Wild quails have the reputation of being so stupid that they never run away from hunters, but stay rooted to the spot as sitting targets. As a result, they have become very rare, and most of the birds now available are farmed. They are very small (you need two to serve one person) and have a delicate, subtly gamey flavor. Farmed quails have less flavor than the wild birds and benefit from added flavorings, such as grapes.

Quail
These birds have a very delicate, gamey flavor. They are very small, and so you will need to serve two per person.

Faraona (guinea fowl)

Guinea fowl are extremely decorative birds with luxuriant gray-and-white spotted plumage. They originated in West Africa, but are now farmed all over Europe, so that although they are technically game, they are classified as poultry. They taste similar to chicken, but have a firmer texture and a more robust flavor.

COOKING GUINEA FOWL

Although their abundant plumage makes them seem larger, guinea fowl are only about the size of a small spring chicken, so one bird will not feed more than three people. To roast guinea fowl, wrap the breasts with bacon slices and roast like chicken, basting frequently. A vegetable stuffing will keep the flesh moist. Guinea fowl can be substituted for chicken or turkey in any recipe.

CULINARY USES

Guinea fowl are hugely popular in Italy, where they are served in much the same ways as chicken. The flesh of an adult guinea fowl is firmer than that of a chicken, so it is best to wrap it or cover the breasts with bacon slices before roasting. The breasts are sometimes sautéed and served with the pan juices mixed with balsamic vinegar, or with a sauce of cream and Marsala. The birds can be roasted or pot-roasted whole, or cut into serving pieces and casseroled with mushrooms (wild mushrooms are especially delicious) or herbs. A favorite autumn dish in Tuscany is guinea fowl braised with chestnuts.

Guinea fowl
These popular birds can be pot-roasted, roasted or casseroled with wild mushrooms

Piccione (pigeon)

Wood pigeons have dark, gamey flesh and a robust flavor, which the Italians love. They are generally too tough to roast, but they make the most delicious casseroles. Domestic pigeons are also reared for food and you will often see large dovecotes in farmyards. Domestic birds are less likely to be tough than wild ones, but their flavor is less robust.

Wild pigeon
Italians love the rich, robust flavor of these small birds; however, they can be very tough, so cook them very slowly, either by braising or casseroling

COOKING PIGEONS

Wild pigeons can be tough, so, unless you are sure that they are young, it is best to casserole them. In Tuscany, they are braised with tomatoes and olives; the classic Venetian way is to stew them with pancetta, ox tongue and fresh green peas. If you really want to roast wild pigeons, marinate them in a red wine marinade for three days before cooking, then stuff them with a moist vegetable stuffing. Cover the breasts with fatty bacon and roast for about 20 minutes, basting with the marinade every few minutes.

Fish & Shellfish

Italy's extensive coastal waters once teemed with a huge variety of fish and shellfish, many unique to that part of the Adriatic and Mediterranean. Sadly, pollution and over-fishing have taken their toll, and there is no longer the abundance of seafood there once was, but what remains is of excellent quality. A visit to an Italian fish market will reveal fish and shellfish of every description, some beautiful, some hideous, many unknown outside Italy. Italians like their seafood very fresh and tend to cook it simply, without elaborate sauces. Large fish are usually plainly grilled or baked and dressed with olive oil, or baked in cartoccio (enclosed in a paper bag). Small shellfish are deep-fried for a crisp fritto misto di mare. Every coastal area has its own version of fish soup, which uses a mixture of local fish and constitutes a meal in itself—cacciucco from Livorno, cold burrida from Sardinia, brodetto from the Adriatic coast— each region claims that its version is the best.

It is impossible to give a complete list of all the fish that you will find in Italy. Popular favorites include *coda di rospo* (monkfish), *dentice* (dentex—a white-fleshed fish found only in Italy), *sogliola* (sole) and even non-indigenous fish such as salmon.

Freshwater fish—trout, perch, carp and eels—abound in the lakes and rivers and are eaten with gusto. Eels are regarded as a particular delicacy and are cooked in many different ways, from grilling to baking, stewing and frying.

Some fish are dried, salted or preserved in oil. The most popular is tuna, which is packed in olive oil and sold by weight from huge cans. *Baccalà* is salted dried cod, which is creamed to a rich paste or made into soups and stews. Anchovies are salted, or packed in olive oil, or preserved in a sweet and sour marinade. Sardines are also very popular and are used to make a Sicilian pasta sauce.

Anchovies
Canned in olive oil (above) or salted (left)—these tiny, strong-tasting fish are used to add flavor to pasta sauces and salads

Salt cod *(baccalà)*
This dried fish is creamed to a paste or made into soups and stews

CHOOSING FRESH FISH

You can almost guarantee that any fish you buy in an Italian early morning market will be ultra-fresh, but at fishmongers and restaurants you should look for pointers. Fish should have bright, slightly bulging eyes and shiny, faintly slimy skin. Open up the gills to check that they are clear red or dark pink and prod the fish lightly to check that the flesh is springy. All fish should have only a faint, pleasant smell; you can tell a stale fish a mile off by its unpleasant odor.

Orata (gilt-head sea bream)

This Mediterranean fish takes its name from the crescent-shaped golden mark on its domed head and the gold spots on each cheek. It has beautiful silvery scales and slightly coarse but delicious flaky white flesh. Orate usually weigh between 1 lb 6 oz and 2¼ lb; a larger fish will serve two greedy people. Orata is best simply broiled, baked *in cartoccio* or barbecued.

Pesce spada (swordfish)

In Italy, you will occasionally find a whole swordfish on the fishmonger's slab. These huge Mediterranean fish, up to 15 feet long and weighing 220–1200 lb, are immediately recognizable by their long sword-like upper jaw. Because of their size, they are more usually sold cut into steaks. Their firm, close-grained, almost meaty flesh has given them a nickname of "steak of the sea."

COOKING SWORDFISH

Swordfish tends to be dry, so it should be marinated in oil and lemon juice or wine and herbs before cooking. It is excellent grilled or barbecued, or part-cooked in butter or olive oil, then baked in a sauce. Its firm texture makes it ideal for kebabs. It is plentiful in the waters around Sicily, where it is cooked with traditional Mediterranean ingredients such as tomatoes, olives, capers, raisins and pine nuts. Another popular Sicilian dish is braciole di pesce spada, *thin slices of swordfish rolled around a stuffing of bread crumbs, mozzarella and herbs and grilled. It is also delicious sliced wafer-thin, marinated in olive oil, lemon juice and herbs and served raw.*

Swordfish
Often either baked or grilled, this firm-fleshed fish needs to be marinated to keep it moist during cooking

Tuna
Immensely popular throughout Italy, canned tuna in oil is either sold by weight from huge cans or bought in small cans like these

TONNO ALL'OLIO D'OLIVA

NOSTROMO

TONNO
DI PRIMA SCELTA

300 g

Fish

Sarde or sardelle (sardines)

Fresh sardines probably take their name from Sardinia, where they were once abundant. These small, silvery fish are still found in Mediterranean waters, where they grow to about 5 in. They are at their best in spring. Allow about four larger sardines or six smaller fish per serving. Sardines have very oily flesh and should only be eaten when extremely fresh. They can also be bought preserved in oil or salt.

Sardines
These fish are at their best in the spring

PREPARING AND COOKING SARDINES

Sardines should be gutted before cooking. If the fishmonger has not already done this, cut the head almost through to the backbone and pull it off; the gut will come away with the head.

Sardines can be barbecued, broiled or baked alla genovese with fresh potatoes, garlic and parsley. Their oily flesh combines well with spices and tart ingredients such as capers and olives. In Sicily they are stuffed with bread crumbs, pine nuts, raisins and anchovies and fried, then finished in the oven (a beccaficcu). Sardines can also be deep-fried, either plain or stuffed with mushrooms, herbs and cheese (alla ligure) or with chopped spinach and cream (alla romana).

Spigola or branzino (sea bass)

The silvery sea bass, which come from Mediterranean waters, are as beautiful to look at as to eat, although their rapacious nature has earned them the nickname of "sea wolf." These slim, elegant fish are almost always sold whole and rarely weigh much more than 2¼ lb, so one fish will feed no more than two or three people. Sea bass is prized for its delicate white flesh and lack of irritating small bones. As a result, it is never cheap.

One way of bringing the price down is to farm sea bass, but the flavor of the farmed fish is not as fine as that of wild sea bass, whose predatory habits ensure that their flesh develops a full flavor. So far, farming of these wonderful fish does not seem to have caught on in Italy, where flavor is rarely compromised for cost.

PREPARING AND COOKING SEA BASS

Sea bass should be gutted before cooking. They have quite hard scales, which should be removed before grilling or pan-frying. Scale the fish with a de-scaler or blunt knife, working from the tail toward the head. If you are going to poach or bake sea bass, leave the scales on, as they will hold the fragile flesh together.
Sea bass has rather soft flesh, so it is best broiled, barbecued or pan-fried and dressed with a trickle of olive oil. It can be stuffed with sprigs of fresh herbs (fennel is particularly good) and baked for 20–30 minutes, depending on the size of the fish. For spigola alla livornese, lay the fish in an ovenproof dish on a layer of rich tomato sauce, sprinkle with seasoned bread crumbs and olive oil and bake.

Triglia (red mullet)

These small Mediterranean fish rarely weigh more than 2¼ lb. They have bright rose-colored skin and a faint golden streak along their sides. Their flesh is succulent with a distinctive, almost shrimp-like flavor, quite unlike any other fish. The liver of red mullet is regarded as a great delicacy and is not removed during cooking, which gives the mullet its nickname of "sea woodcock." Red mullet are extremely perishable and should be eaten the day they are bought. The skin should always look very bright; dullness is a sure indication that the fish is not fresh.

PREPARING AND COOKING RED MULLET

Larger fish should be scaled before cooking, but be warned—this is a delicate operation, as the skin is very fragile. Scaling is worth the effort, however, as it reveals the wonderful red skin in all its glory. Red mullet combines well with traditional Mediterranean flavors of olive oil, black olives, herbs, garlic, saffron and tomatoes. It can be baked, grilled or cooked in cartoccio with powerful herbs such as rosemary or fennel. For triglia all'italiana, *place whole red mullet on a bed of finely chopped mushrooms and onions that have been sweated until soft and mixed with fresh bread crumbs, and bake for 20–30 minutes.*

Red mullet
The flesh of these pretty fish has a distinctive almost shrimp-like flavor

Sea bass
Prized for their delicate white flesh, these slim, elegant fish are almost always sold whole

Shellfish

Italian coastal waters are host to a huge variety of shellfish and crustaceans, many with wonderfully exotic names such as *datteri di mare* (sea dates; a kind of mussel), *tartufi di mare* (sea truffles; a type of clam) and *fragolino di mare* (sea strawberry; a tiny octopus that turns bright pink when cooked). Almost all seafood is considered edible, from clams to *cannolicchi* (razor-shells), *lumache di mare* (sea snails) and *canestrelli* (small scallops). Shrimps come in all sizes and colors, from vibrant red to pale gray, while crustaceans range from bright orange crawfish to blue-black lobsters.

COOKING SQUID AND CUTTLEFISH

Small squid and cuttlefish should be cooked only briefly— just until they turn opaque—or they will become rubbery and tough.
Larger specimens need long, slow cooking to make them tender. They can be stuffed with ground fish or meat, anchovies and seasoned bread crumbs or rice, baked with tomatoes and wine sauce until tender, or cut into rings and fried in a light batter or simply dusted with seasoned flour and deep-fried. Squid and cuttlefish are also delicious stewed in their own ink; seal the mollusks in hot oil with some chopped onions and garlic, add finely chopped fresh parsley and seasoning, then cover with dry white wine and a little water and simmer gently for 15 minutes. Crush the ink sacs, mix the inky liquid with a little cold water and 2–3 tbsp flour and work into a smooth paste. Add the flour mixture to the pan and cook for another 5–10 minutes.

Squid
Large specimens such as this one need long, slow cooking to make them tender—conversely, small baby squid should be cooked very quickly or they will become tough

Calamari or totani (squid) and seppie (cuttlefish)

Despite their appearance, squid and cuttlefish are actually mollusks whose shell is located inside the body. They are indistinguishable in taste, but cuttlefish have a larger head and a wider body with stubbier tentacles. The cuttlebone, much loved by parrots, is the bone of the cuttlefish inside the body. Once this has been removed, cuttlefish are very tender. The "shell" of a squid is nothing more than a long, thin, transparent quill. Both *seppie* and *calamari* have ten tentacles.

Squid and cuttlefish are immensely popular in Italy, cut into rings and served as part of either an *insalata di mare* (seafood salad) or *fritto misto* (mixed fried fish). Their black ink is used to flavor and color risotto and fresh pasta.

PREPARING AND COOKING MUSSELS

Scrub the shells under cold running water. Pull off the "beard" protruding from the shell. Give any open mussels a sharp tap; they should close immediately. Discard any that do not, as they are probably dead.
The simplest way to cook mussels is alla marinara. *For 4 people, finely chop 1 large onion, 2 garlic cloves and 1 tbsp chopped parsley, put in a large pan with 2¼ cups white wine and simmer for 5 minutes. Add the scrubbed mussels, cover and steam, shaking the pan occasionally, for 5 minutes, or until the shells have opened. Discard any unopened mussels, sprinkle the rest with extra parsley and serve. For a richer sauce, transfer the mussels to a bowl and reduce the sauce over high heat. Pour it over the shellfish and serve.*

PREPARING SQUID

You can usually buy squid already cleaned, but failing that, it is easy to prepare it yourself. Hold the body in one hand and the head in the other, and pull the head gently but firmly. The soft entrails will come away cleanly. Cut off the tentacles and remove the dark ink sac from the head.

Pull out the transparent quill and rinse the body inside and out. Peel off the purplish membrane. Unless the squid are tiny enough to serve whole, cut the body into ¼ in rings and the tentacles into manageable pieces.

Polipi *(octopus)*

These are much larger than squid and have only eight tentacles. Their ink sac is not located in the head but in their liver, and the ink has a strong, pungent taste. Octopus look and taste similar to squid, but need a good deal of preparation. They must be pounded (99 times, some say) to tenderize them before they are subjected to very long, slow cooking.

If you can find very small octopus, they can be cooked in the same way as squid, but otherwise it is less trouble to substitute squid or cuttlefish.

Octopus
When small, these can be cooked like squid

Cozze *(mussels)*

Mussels, with their smooth texture and sweet flavor, make an attractive addition to many pasta and fish dishes. Pollution in the Mediterranean has threatened the indigenous mussel population, so nowadays most Italian mussels are farmed by the *bouchot* method, on ropes attached to long stakes set in pure seawater, which keeps the mollusks clean and healthy and free from grit and sand. In Italian fish markets on the Adriatic coast, you may find small sweet local mussels with different names like *peoci* or *datteri di mare*. These can be prepared in the same way as other mussels.

CHOOSING

Mussels, sold by the litre in Italy, are very inexpensive. Because the shells constitute so much of the weight, allow at least a generous 2½ cups mussels per serving. Choose those that feel heavy for their size and discard any with broken shells. Use mussels the day they are gathered or bought.

Mussels
Steamed mussels combine well with black fettuccine or tagliatelle

CULINARY USES

Once mussels have been steamed open, they can be served with a garlicky tomato sauce, or baked on the half shell with garlic butter or a bread crumb topping. For *cozze gratinate al forno*, lay the mussels on the bottom shells in an ovenproof dish, sprinkle lavishly with bread crumbs seasoned with garlic and parsley and drizzle with olive oil. Bake for 10 minutes.

Shelled cooked mussels are combined with shrimp and squid for an *insalata di mare* (seafood salad), or used as a pizza topping, while mussels in the shell are often mixed with other seafood and pasta for dishes like *spaghetti allo scoglio* ("spaghetti of the rock").

Shellfish

Gamberetti, gamberelli and gamberoni (shrimp)

There are so many different varieties of shrimp in Italian coastal waters that it is almost impossible to recognize them all. The smallest are the *gamberetti*, small pink or brown shrimps that are usually boiled and served simply dressed with olive oil and lemon juice as part of an *antipasto*. Next in size come the *gamberelli*, pink shrimp with a delicate flavor. These are the shrimp that are most commonly used in a *fritto misto di mare* (mixed fried seafood). *Gamberi rossi* are the larger variety of shrimp, which turn bright red when they are cooked. They are highly prized for their fine, strong flavor, and are eaten plainly cooked and dipped into a bowl of *maionese* (mayonnaise). Best (and most expensive) of all are *gamberoni*, large succulent shrimp from the Adriatic, which have a superb flavor and texture. Similar to these is the *cicala*, which resembles a small flattish lobster.

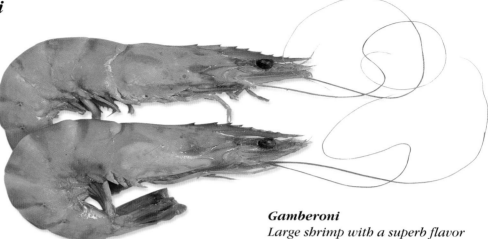

Gamberoni
Large shrimp with a superb flavor

COOKING SHRIMP

Whatever the size, all types of shrimp can be cooked briefly in boiling salted water (sea water, if possible) until they turn pink. Medium shrimp will take only 1–2 minutes, large shrimp up to 5 minutes. The robust flavor of shrimp makes them ideal for serving in a rich tomato or cream sauce or with rice. Shell them after cooking. To grill gamberoni, rub the shells with olive oil and coarse salt and grill over charcoal or on a grilling pan, turning them frequently. When they turn opaque, slit them through the underside and open them out flat like a butterfly. Brush the underside with oil and grill until just cooked. Peeled shrimp can be pan-fried in olive oil flavored with garlic and/or chili, parsley and capers or coated in batter or egg and bread crumbs and deep-fried.

Gamberi rossi
These large shrimp turn bright red when cooked

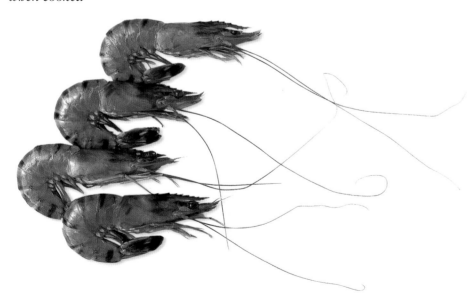

PREPARING SHRIMP

Shrimp should be deveined before or after cooking. Pull off the heads, shell the tails and pick out the black thread-like intestine with a knife tip.

CHOOSING

Almost all the shrimp you buy in Italy are sold uncooked. They should have bright shells that feel firm; if they look limp or smell of ammonia, do not buy them.

CULINARY USES

Shrimp are extremely versatile and can be used in a wide variety of dishes. Small shrimps are served as *antipasti*, either on their own, or as a stuffing for tomatoes. They can be added to risotto and pasta dishes or seafood sauces.

Larger shrimp combine well with almost any other seafood. They are usually included in an *insalata di mare* (seafood salad) or *fritto misto di mare* (mixed fried seafood). They make a fine *antipasto* added to an *insalata russa* (Russian salad) or served with green beans dressed with extra virgin olive oil. They combine well with a spicy tomato sauce or mushrooms, and can be used for seafood casseroles. Large shrimp can be skewered or split and grilled, or boiled and served with mayonnaise or lemon.

Gamberetti
These small pink shrimps are delicious simply dressed with olive oil and lemon juice

Vongole (clams)

There are almost as many different types of clam as there are regions in Italy, ranging from tiny smooth-shelled *arselle* or *vongole* to long thin razor shells and the large Venus clams with beautiful ridged shells called *tartufi di mare* ("sea truffles"). All have a sweet flavor and a slightly chewy texture. Because they vary so much in size, it is best to ask the fishmonger how many clams you will need for a particular dish.

Clams
These smooth-shelled vongole *are often steamed and served as part of a seafood salad*

PREPARING AND COOKING CLAMS

Their habit of burying themselves in the sand makes clams rather gritty, so they should be left in fresh water for an hour or so to open up and disgorge the sand inside the shells. To open large clams, either use an oyster knife, or put them in a medium oven for a few minutes until they gape open.

Clams can be served raw like oysters, or cooked in exactly the same way as mussels (see page 70). The cooking time depends on the size of the clams; tiny specimens take only a minute or two. Steamed shelled clams are often served as part of an insalata di mare *or in a risotto. Miniature clams in their shells are stewed with olive oil, garlic and parsley and served with their juices (*in bianco*) or used in a tomato sauce (*in rosso*) for* spaghetti alle vongole, *or served on fried bread as* crostini. *Large varieties can be pan-fried with lemon and parsley, or stuffed with seasoned bread crumbs and grilled or baked.*

Vegetables

Vegetables have always played a very important role in Italian cooking, particularly in the south of the country, where meat was a luxury that few could afford. They are most often served as dishes in their own right, rather than accompaniments, and the range of imaginative vegetable recipes from all over Italy seems infinite.

One of the great joys of Italy is shopping at the markets, where an astonishing range of seasonal vegetables is on display, from asparagus, beans and *cavolo nero* from the north to eggplants, peppers and zucchini from Calabria and Sicily. In spring and summer, you will find at least ten different varieties of lettuce, and you will be overwhelmed by the aroma of freshly picked local tomatoes still on the vine. Italians almost never buy imported or out-of-season vegetables, but prefer to purchase fresh seasonal produce bursting with flavor.

Asparagi (asparagus)

Asparagus has been grown commercially in northeastern Italy for over 300 years and is still highly prized as a luxury vegetable. It has a short growing season from April to early June and is really only worth eating during this period. Both green and white asparagus are cultivated in Italy; the green variety is grown above ground so that the entire spear is bright green. They are harvested when they are about 6 in high. The fat white spears with their pale yellow tips are grown under mounds of soil to protect them from the light, and harvested almost as soon as the tips appear above the soil to retain their pale color. Both varieties have a delicious fresh grassy flavor.

CULINARY USES

In spring, Italians enjoy young asparagus spears simply boiled, steamed or roasted in olive oil and served as a *primo* (first course) with butter and freshly grated Parmesan. For an extra treat, they add a fried egg and dip the asparagus tips into

White asparagus
This variety is grown under mounds of earth to retain the pale color

Green asparagus
Enjoyed by Italians, simply boiled or roasted in olive oil

the creamy yolk. When served as a vegetable accompaniment, asparagus can be crisply fried in egg and bread crumbs. The tips also make a luxury addition to risotto.

BUYING AND STORING

Asparagus starts to lose its flavor as soon as it has been cut, so be sure to buy only the freshest spears. The best guide is the tips, which should be firm and tight. If they are drooping and open, the asparagus is past its best. The stalks should be straight and fresh-looking, not yellowed and shriveled or very woody at the base. Allow about eight medium spears per serving as a first course and always buy spears of uniform thickness so that they cook evenly. Asparagus will keep in the vegetable compartment of the refrigerator for two or three days.

PREPARING AND COOKING ASPARAGUS

Freshly cut garden asparagus needs no trimming, but cut off at least ¾ in from the bottom of the stalks of bought spears until the exposed end looks fresh and moist. Peel the lower half with a potato peeler. (You need not do this for very thin stalks.)

Boiling asparagus can be problematic, since the stalks take longer to cook than the tips. The ideal solution is to use a special asparagus kettle, so as to immerse the stalks in boiling water while steaming the tips.

Asparagus can also be stood upright in a deep pan of boiling water, tented with foil and cooked for 5–8 minutes, until tender but still al dente. *Alternatively, steam the spears in a vegetable steamer. Serve with a drizzle of extra virgin olive oil or melted butter.*

Asparagus can also be successfully microwaved. Wash the spears and lay them in an oval dish in a single layer with the tips all pointing the same way. You need not add water. Cover tightly with plastic wrap and cook on full power for 5 minutes per 1¼ lb. If the spears are not quite done, turn them over and cook for a little longer.

To roast asparagus, heat some olive oil in a roasting pan, turn the spears in the oil, then roast in a hot oven for 5–10 minutes.

To fry, roll the spears in beaten egg and fine dried bread crumbs, then fry them a few at a time in very hot olive oil until crusty and golden. Drain on paper towel and sprinkle with sea salt.

Cardi (cardoons)

Cardoons are related to artichokes, but only the leaf-stalks are eaten. They are commercially grown in mounds of soil to keep them creamy white, but in the wild, the stalks are pale green and hairy and can grow to an enormous size. The tough outer stalks are always discarded, and only the inner stalks and hearts are eaten. Cardoons are a popular winter vegetable in Italy and can be found in the markets ready-trimmed.

CULINARY USES

Cardoons can be eaten raw as a salad, or cooked in a variety of ways—fried, puréed or boiled and served with melted butter or a rich cream and Parmesan sauce. They are traditionally used as a vegetable to dip into the hot anchovy and garlic fondue known as *bagna cauda*.

BUYING AND STORING

Cardoons bought at the market will have been trimmed of their outer stalks and are sold with a crown of leaves, like large heads of celery. The stalks should be plump and creamy-white and not too hairy. Wrapped in a plastic bag, they will keep in the vegetable compartment of the refrigerator for two or three days.

PREPARING AND COOKING CARDOONS

Cut off the roots and peel the stalks with a potato peeler to remove the stringy fibers. Cut the stalks into 2½ in lengths and the hearts into wedges, and drop into acidulated water to prevent discoloration.

Blanch in boiling salted water, then simmer or fry gently in butter until tender. To serve in a sauce, put the blanched cardoons in an ovenproof dish, cover with sauce, sprinkle with grated Parmesan and broil until browned.

Cardoons
Related to artichokes, the tough outer stalks of this vegetable are always discarded

Vegetables

Carciofi (artichokes)

As their appearance suggests, artichokes are a type of thistle. Originating from Sicily, where they grow almost wild, they are cultivated throughout Italy and are a particular specialty of Roman cooking. The artichoke itself is actually the flower bud of the large, silvery-leaved plant. There are many different varieties, from tiny purple plants with tapered leaves, which are so tender that they can be eaten raw, to large bright or pale green globes, whose leaves are pulled off one by one and the succulent flesh at the base stripped off with your teeth.

HISTORY

Although artichokes have always grown like weeds in Sicily, they were first cultivated near Naples in the fifteenth century. Their popularity spread to Florence, where they became a favorite dish of the Medici family. They were believed to have powerful properties as an aphrodisiac and women were often forbidden to eat them!

CULINARY USES

Tiny tender artichokes can be quartered and eaten raw or braised *alla romana* with olive oil, parsley and garlic. Large specimens can be served boiled with a dressing to dip the leaves into, or stuffed with savory fillings. They can be cut into wedges, dipped in batter and deep-fried. A favorite Italian dish is the ancient Jewish recipe *carciofi alla giudea*, where the artichokes are flattened out and deep-fried twice, so that the outside is very crisp while the inside remains meltingly moist.

BUYING AND STORING

Artichokes are available almost all year round, but they are at their best in summer. Whichever variety you are buying, look for tightly packed leaves (open leaves indicate that they are too mature) and a very fresh color. When an artichoke is old, the tips of the leaves will turn brown. If possible, buy artichokes still attached to their stems; they will stay fresher and the

peeled, cooked stems are often as delicious as the artichoke itself.

Artichokes will stay fresh for several days if you place the stalks in water like a bunch of flowers. If they have no stalks, wrap them in plastic wrap and keep in the vegetable compartment of the refrigerator for a day or two.

PREPARING AND COOKING ARTICHOKES

Tiny tender artichokes can be quartered and eaten raw.

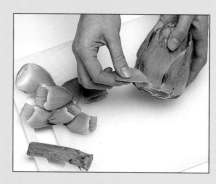

For large artichokes, snap off the stalk and pull off the tough outer leaves. Rub the cut surfaces with lemon juice to prevent discoloration and keep the prepared artichokes in a bowl of acidulated water until ready to cook.

Boil large whole artichokes for about 30 minutes, until the outer leaves can be pulled off easily.

Drain them upside-down, then pull out the center leaves and scoop out the inedible hairy choke with a spoon before serving. For stuffed artichokes, remove the choke before cooking and fill the cavity with your chosen stuffing. Braise them in olive oil and water, or invert them onto an ovenproof dish, pour on a mixture of olive oil and water, cover with foil and bake at 375°F for about 1 hour.

Very small artichokes should be quartered and boiled, braised or stewed until tender. The chokes are so soft that the artichokes can be eaten whole.

Artichokes
These popular vegetables are actually the flower bud of a type of large thistle

Cavolo (cabbage)

Cabbage is an essential ingredient of many Italian hearty winter soups. Three main types are used: *cavolo verza* (curly-leaved savoy cabbage), which is used in Milanese dishes, *cavolo cappuccio* (round white or red cabbage) and the specialty of Tuscany, *cavolo nero*, a tall leafy cabbage whose name means "black cabbage," but which is actually dark purplish green.

CULINARY USES

Italians rarely eat cabbage as a vegetable side dish, but prefer to include it in hearty soups, such as *ribollita* or minestrone, or to stuff and braise the outer leaves and serve them as a main course.

BUYING AND STORING

Cabbage heads should be solid and firm, with fresh, unyellowed leaves. It is best to buy them complete with their outer leaves; not only are these tasty for cooking, but they protect the hearts and give a good indication of the freshness of the cabbage. A cabbage will keep in the vegetable compartment of the refrigerator for up to a week.

Cavolo nero
The name of this tall leafy cabbage means "black cabbage"

Red and white cabbage
The red variety is often cooked gently with apples and spices to serve with rich meats, while the white variety is added to soups and stews

Savoy cabbage
This curly-leaved cabbage is used in Milanese dishes

PREPARING AND COOKING CABBAGE

Cut off the outer leaves and stalk, cutting out a cone-shaped section of the stalk from the inside of the cabbage. To use the leaves for stuffing, blanch them in boiling water for about 3 minutes, until malleable. For soups and braised dishes, coarsely shred the cabbage and wash it well.

Cabbage can be cooked in a variety of ways. The simplest cooking method is to toss shredded cabbage in butter or olive oil until just tender. Never overcook cabbage; it should still retain some crunch.

Winter cabbages are good shredded and braised with pancetta *and garlic, while* cavolo rosso *(red cabbage) can be spiced with apples, cinnamon and cloves and stewed in a little white wine to cut the richness of pork, duck or roast goose.*

Vegetables

Cipolle (onions)

Onions are an essential part of Italian cooking. Many varieties are grown, including mild yellow onions, the stronger-flavored white onions and their baby version, which is used for pickling and sweet-and-sour onions. The best-known Italian onions are the vibrant deep red variety, which are delicious raw (in a tuna and bean salad, for example), or cooked.

CULINARY USES

The best Italian onions are grown in Piedmont, so many classic Piedmontese recipes include these versatile bulbs. Large onions can be stuffed with Fontina or ground meat and herbs, and baked. Baby white onions are traditionally cooked *in agrodolce*, a sweet-and-sour sauce of sugar and wine vinegar, and served cold as an *antipasto* or hot as a vegetable accompaniment.

BUYING AND STORING

You will often find young fresh onions in Italian markets. These are sold in bunches like large, bulbous scallions, complete with their leaves. They have a mild flavor and can be used for pickling or in salads. They will keep in the refrigerator for three or four days; wrap them to prevent their smell from pervading everything else in the refrigerator. Older onions have thin, almost papery skins that should be unblemished. The onions should feel firm and not be sprouting green leaves. They quickly deteriorate once cut, so it is best to buy assorted sizes, then you can use a small onion when the recipe calls for only a small amount. Stored in a dry, airy place, onions will keep for many weeks.

White onion
This variety is very strongly flavored

Red onion
This vibrant red variety is now widely available—they are delicious raw

Baby white onions
Traditionally cooked in agrodolce, *a classic Italian sweet-and-sour sauce, and served cold as an* antipasto

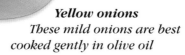

Yellow onions
These mild onions are best cooked gently in olive oil

PREPARING AND COOKING ONIONS

Some onions are easier to peel than others. The skins of red and yellow onions can be removed without much difficulty, but white onions may need to be plunged into boiling water for about 30 seconds to make peeling easier.

There are all sorts of old wives' remedies to prevent your eyes from watering when peeling onions. The most effective method is to hold them as far away from you as possible while you peel. For most cooked dishes, onions should be sliced or chopped, but for salads they are sliced into very thin rings.

The flavor of onions will develop in different ways, according to how you cook them. In Italian cooking, they are rarely browned, which gives them a bitter taste, but are generally sweated gently in olive oil to add a mellow flavor to a multitude of dishes.

Finocchio *(fennel)*

Originally a medicinal remedy for such disagreeable conditions as flatulence, fennel has become one of the most important of all Italian vegetables. Bulb or Florence fennel (so-called to distinguish it from the feathery green herb) resembles a fat white celery root and has a delicate but distinctive flavor of aniseed and a very crisp, refreshing texture.

CULINARY USES

Fennel is delicious eaten raw, dressed with a vinaigrette or as part of a mixed salad. In southern Italy, raw fennel is served with cheese as a dessert instead of fruit—an excellent aid to digesting a meal.

When cooked, the aniseed flavor becomes more subtle and the texture resembles cooked celery. Braised fennel is particularly good with white fish. Fennel can be cooked in all the same ways as celery or cardoons.

BUYING AND STORING

Fennel is available all year round. If possible, buy it with its topknot of feathery green fronds, which you can chop and use as an herb or garnish in any dish where you would use dill. The bulbs should feel firm and the outer layers should be crisp and white, not shriveled and yellowish. It should have a delicate, very fresh scent of aniseed and the crisp texture of green celery. Whole fennel bulbs will keep in the refrigerator for up to a week. Once cut, however, use them immediately, or the cut surfaces will discolor and the texture will soften. Allow a whole bulb per serving.

Fennel
The distinctive aniseed flavor makes this vegetable a perfect partner for white fish

PREPARING AND COOKING FENNEL

If the outer layer of the fennel bulb seems stringy, peel it with a sharp knife. Cut off the round greenish stalks protruding from the top. For salads, cut the bulb vertically into thin slices. For cooked dishes, quarter the bulb. Any trimmings can be chopped and used for soups or sauces for fish.

Fennel can be sautéed, baked or braised. For all cooked fennel recipes, blanch the quartered bulbs in a large saucepan of salted boiling water until it is just tender.

To sauté, heat about 2 tbsp butter per bulb with some chopped garlic, drain the fennel and fry it gently in the butter until very tender. To enhance the flavor, add a teaspoon of Pernod or other aniseed-flavored alcohol.

Braised fennel should be cooked in a little olive oil using a covered frying pan.

To bake fennel, lay the blanched bulbs in a buttered ovenproof dish, season, dot with butter and sprinkle a generous quantity of freshly grated Parmesan over the top. Bake at 400°F for 20–30 minutes or until the top is bubbling and golden brown.

Vegetables

Melanzane (eggplants)

The versatile eggplant plays an important role in the cooking of southern Italy and Sicily, possibly because its dense, satisfying texture makes a good substitute for meat. You will find many different eggplants in Italian markets, the two main types being the familiar deep purple elongated variety and the rotund paler mauve type, which has a thinner skin. Some are small, some huge, but they all taste similar and can be used in the same way for any recipe.

PREPARING EGGPLANTS

Some people believe that eggplants should always be sliced and salted for about 30 minutes before cooking to draw out the bitter juices; others deem this unnecessary. Salting does prevent eggplant from soaking up large quantities of oil during cooking, so it is probably worth doing.

Slice or dice the eggplants, place them in a colander, sprinkle with 1 tbsp salt per 2¼ lb. Place a dish on the eggplants and weight it down. Set aside for 30 minutes. Rinse the eggplants and dry with paper towels.

If eggplants have a very tough skin, it is best to peel them (unless you are stuffing them and need the skin as a container). Otherwise, leave the skin on, as its color will enhance the appearance of the finished dish.

BUYING AND STORING

Shape and size are not important when choosing eggplants; the essentials are tight, glossy skins and a fairly firm texture. Do not buy eggplants with wrinkled or damaged skins. They should feel heavy for their size; a light eggplant will probably be spongy inside and contain a lot of seeds. They will keep in the refrigerator for up to a week.

Eggplants
The familiar deep purple variety plays an important role in the cooking of southern Italy

HISTORY

Eggplants originated in Asia. They were cultivated in Europe in the Middle Ages, but only very rarely featured in Italian cooking at the time, since they were regarded with suspicion; indeed, the name *melanzane* comes from the Latin *melum insanum* (unhealthy apple). This mistrust had been overcome by the Renaissance, and eggplants began to be grown and used extensively in the south of Italy.

CULINARY USES

Eggplants are extremely versatile vegetables and add a wonderful depth of flavor to any dish in which they appear. They can be broiled, baked, stuffed, stewed and sautéed, on their own or with other ingredients, and the rich color of their skins enhances the appearance of many different Italian dishes.

COOKING EGGPLANTS

*The simplest way of cooking eggplants is to slice and fry them in a generous quantity of very hot olive oil.
For a more substantial dish, coat them in light batter, then fine bread crumbs, and fry until golden brown.
To bake them, halve the eggplants lengthwise, removing the calyx and stalk. Make slashes in the flesh and rub it with a cut garlic clove. Drizzle some olive oil over the top, cover with foil and bake for about 1 hour, until very soft. Season with salt and pepper and add lemon juice to taste.
Probably the most famous Italian eggplant dish is* melanzane alla parmigiana, *where the eggplants are layered with rich tomato sauce and Parmesan and baked. A favorite Sicilian dish,* caponata, *combines them with celery and a piquant sweet-and-sour sauce enlivened with olives and sometimes capers.*

Peperoni (bell peppers)

Generically known as capsicums, the shape of these peppers gives them the alternative name of "bell peppers." Although they come in a range of colors—green (these are unripe red peppers), red, yellow, orange and even purplish-black—all peppers have much the same sweetish flavor and crunchy texture, and are interchangeable in recipes. They are a very healthy food, being rich in Vitamin C. The locally grown peppers you will see in the markets in Italy are much larger and more misshapen than the uniformly perfect, hydroponically grown specimens but their flavor is sweet and delicious.

CULINARY USES

Each region of Italy has its own specialties using peppers. They can be used raw or lightly roasted in salads or as an *antipasto* and can be cooked in a variety of ways—roasted and dressed with olive oil or vinaigrette dressing and capers, stewed (as in *peperonata*), or stuffed and baked. Peppers have a great affinity with other Mediterranean ingredients, such as olives, capers, eggplants, tomatoes and anchovies.

BUYING AND STORING

Choose firm peppers with unwrinkled, shiny skins. Size does not matter unless you plan to stuff the peppers, in which case choose roundish shapes of uniform size. The skin of green peppers may be mottled with patches of orange or red; this indicates that the pepper is ripening, and as long as the pepper is unblemished, there is no reason not to buy it. Peppers can be stored in the fridge for up to two weeks.

COOKING PEPPERS

To make a classic Italian peperonata, *sweat sliced onions and garlic in olive oil, add sliced peppers, cover the pan and cook gently until just tender. Add an equal quantity of peeled, deseeded and chopped tomatoes, a splash of wine vinegar and seasoning and cook, uncovered, until meltingly tender. For* peperonata alla romana, *stir in some capers at the end.*

Peppers
Locally grown Italian peppers are often larger and more misshapen than the uniformly perfect varieties grown in hot-houses

Vegetables

PREPARING AND COOKING PEPPERS

Place the peppers under a very hot broiler or hold them over a gas flame and turn them until the skin blackens and blisters. Put them in a plastic bag, seal and set aside until the peppers are cool enough to handle. The thin skin will peel off easily.

To slice peppers, halve them lengthwise, cut out the calyx and stem and pull out the core, seeds and white membranes. Cut the flesh into strips.

To stuff peppers, cut off the stalk end and remove the seeds and membranes. Fill the pepper with your chosen stuffing (rice, vegetables, meat—whatever you want) and replace the stalk end. Arrange the peppers in a shallow ovenproof dish, drizzle on some olive oil and pour in enough water to come about ¾ in up the sides of the peppers. Bake at 400°F for about 1 hour.

For baked peppers alla piemontese, halve the peppers lengthwise and fill each with a chopped tomato, a chopped anchovy fillet and a little chopped garlic. Arrange the peppers on a baking tray, rounded side down. Drizzle on some olive oil and bake at 400°F for about 30 minutes.

Pomodori (tomatoes)

It is impossible to imagine Italian cooking without tomatoes, which seem to be a vital ingredient in almost every recipe. But these "golden apples" were unknown in Italy until the sixteenth century, when they were brought over from Mexico. At first they were grown only in the south, but as their popularity spread, tomatoes were cultivated all over Italy and were incorporated into the cooking of every region. Italians grow an enormous variety of tomatoes, from plum tomatoes (San Marzano are the best) to ridged, pumpkin-shaped, green-tinged salad tomatoes, bright red fruits bursting with aroma and flavor, and tiny *pomodorini* (cherry tomatoes).

CULINARY USES

Tomatoes are used in so many different ways that it is hard to know where to begin. They can be eaten raw, sliced and served with a trickle of extra virgin olive oil and some torn basil leaves (basil and tomatoes have an extraordinary affinity). They are the red component of an *insalata tricolore*, partnering white mozzarella and green basil to make

Cherry tomatoes
Bright red and bursting with flavor, these tiny tomatoes can be used to add color and flavor to any dish

Plum tomatoes
San Marzano are the best variety of these smooth-skinned tomatoes

up the colors of the Italian flag. Raw ripe tomatoes can be chopped with herbs and garlic to make a fresh-tasting pasta sauce, or made into a topping for *bruschetta*.

Tomatoes can be broiled, fried, baked, stuffed, stewed and made into sauces and soups. They add color and flavor to almost any savory dish.

BUYING AND STORING

Tomatoes are at their best in summer, when they have ripened naturally in the sun. Choose your tomatoes according to how you wish to prepare them. Salad tomatoes should be very firm and easy to slice. The best tomatoes for cooking are plum tomatoes, which hold their shape well and should have a fine flavor. Tomatoes will only ripen properly if left for long enough on the vine, so try to buy "vine-ripened" varieties. If you can find only unripe

tomatoes, you can ripen them by putting them in a brown paper bag with a ripe tomato or leaving them in a fruit bowl with a banana; the gases the ripe fruits give off will ripen the tomatoes but, alas, they cannot improve the flavor.

Try to buy tomatoes loose so that you can smell them. They should have a wonderful aroma. If the flavor is not all it should be, add a good pinch of sugar to enhance it. For cooked recipes, if you cannot find really flavorful tomatoes, use canned instead. The best are San Marzano plum tomatoes, which are grown near Salerno. In Italy, you will often find large knobby green tomatoes, which are sold as *pomodori da insalata*. Although you can let them ripen in the usual way, Italians prefer to slice these tomatoes thinly and eat them in their unripe state as a crunchy and refreshing salad.

Large tomatoes
Not always as smooth as these, locally grown Italian tomatoes bought at a market can be very ridged and almost pumpkin-shaped

PEELING TOMATOES

It is easy to remove the skin from tomatoes. Prick the tomatoes with the point of a sharp knife, plunge them into a bowl of boiling water for about 30 seconds, then refresh in cold water. Peel away the skins, cut the tomatoes into quarters or halves and remove the seeds using a teaspoon.

Vine-ripened tomatoes
Tomatoes sold on the vine are likely to have a far better flavor than those sold loose

Vegetables

Spinaci (spinach)

Spinach and its close relatives, *bietola* (Swiss chard) and *biete* (spinach beet), are dark green leafy vegetables, rich in minerals (especially iron) and vitamins. Unlike many other vegetables, they are often served in Italy as side dishes to a main course, although they appear in numerous composite dishes as well. All spinach, whether flat-leafed or curly-leafed, has a distinctive metallic flavor, which people either love or loathe. The latter should avoid dishes *alla fiorentina*, which use spinach in large quantities.

Curly-leaf spinach is a summer variety with very dark green leaves. Winter spinach has flat, smooth leaves, but tastes very similar. Usually, only the leaves are eaten and the stalks are discarded. Spinach has a delicate, melting quality and should be cooked only very briefly.

The coarser *bietola* contains less iron and has a less pronounced flavor than spinach. The leaves have broad, tender creamy or pale green midribs, and both the leaves and stalks are eaten, but are cooked in different ways. *Bietola* is available all year round, but is particularly popular in autumn and winter, when more delicate spinach is not available. No one is quite sure why it is called Swiss chard; the Swiss certainly eat it, but in much smaller quantities than the French or Italians.

Biete (spinach beet) has a much smaller stalk and more closely resembles spinach. The stalks are usually left attached to the leaves for cooking. The coarser texture of *biete* makes it more suitable than spinach for recipes that require more than the briefest cooking. Balls of ready-cooked *biete* are often sold in Italian delicatessens.

History

Spinach was originally cultivated in Persia in the sixth century and was brought to Europe by Arab traders some thousand years later. It had become very popular in France, Spain and England by the sixteenth century, when it was used for both sweet and savory dishes, but it did not reach Italy until the eighteenth century.

Culinary Uses

Tender young spinach leaves can be eaten raw in salads or cooked and served cold with a dressing of olive oil and lemon. Cooked spinach is used to make gnocchi and is often combined with ricotta to make fillings for pasta and *crespoline*

Spinach
The tender young leaves can be eaten raw; larger leaves need to be cooked

Spinach beet
The coarse texture of biete *makes it more suitable than spinach for slower-cooked recipes*

(pancakes). Florentine-style recipes usually contain spinach, and it is a classic partner for eggs, fish, poultry and white meats. Spinach, *biete* and *bietola* are all used in savory tarts, such as *torta alla pasqualina*, an Easter speciality. They make excellent soups and soufflés. *Bietola* stalks are delicious sautéed in butter and baked in a white sauce sprinkled with Parmesan.

BUYING AND STORING

All types of spinach should look very fresh and green, with no signs of wilting. The leaves should be unblemished and the stalks crisp. Spinach and spinach beets contain a very high proportion of water and wilt down to about half their weight during cooking, so always buy far more than you think you will need— at least 9 oz per serving. Loose spinach should be used as soon as possible after buying. Packed loosely into a plastic bag, it will keep in the refrigerator for a couple of days. Unopened bags of pre-packaged spinach will keep for up to a week.

Bietola (Swiss chard)

Pull off the green leaves from the stems. Snap the veins and leafstalks and remove the stringy parts (do not cut with a knife, or the strings will not come off). Wash as you would spinach and cut the stalks into 2½–3½ in lengths.

PREPARING AND COOKING SPINACH AND SWISS CHARD

Spinach and spinach beet: Carefully pick over the spinach, discarding any withered or damaged leaves and tough stalks. Wash thoroughly in several changes of water until no signs of earth or grit remain. Spinach should be cooked with only the water that clings to the leaves after washing. Sauté it in butter with a clove of chopped garlic for about 5 minutes; overcooked spinach will be unpleasantly watery. To stew spinach, put it in a large saucepan, cover and cook gently until wilted, turning it over halfway through cooking. Drain and gently squeeze out the excess moisture with your hands. Toss in butter or olive oil, season with freshly grated nutmeg or chop finely and use for gnocchi and pasta fillings.

Swiss chard leaves can be cooked exactly like spinach. The prepared stalks should be blanched until tender in salted water or vegetable stock, then baked in a sauce or tart, sautéed in butter or used as a stuffing. A popular bietola *dish is a* sformato, *a savory, molded, baked custard.*

Swiss chard
Available all year round, this vegetable is particularly popular in winter when the more tender spinach is not available

Vegetables

Zucca (squash) and zucchini

Squashes and zucchini are widely used in northern Italian cooking. Both have large, open, deep-yellow flowers, which are considered a great delicacy. Squashes come in a variety of shapes and sizes, from huge orange pumpkins to small, pale butternut squashes and green acorn squashes. They all have dense, sweet-tasting flesh. Zucchini are especially versatile, with shiny green skin and a sweet, delicate flavor. In Italy, tiny specimens are often sold with their flowers attached.

CULINARY USES

The pumpkin is the symbol of Mantua and recipes *alla mantovana* use the flesh a multitude of ways, from *tortelli alla zucca* (pumpkin-filled tortelli) to risotti, soups and sweet dessert tarts. Pumpkin flowers can be coated in batter and deep-fried, stuffed with a filling of ricotta, or chopped and added to risotti for extra color and flavor.

Zucchini combine well with other Mediterranean vegetables, like tomatoes and eggplants. They can be dipped in batter and deep-fried, made into fritters or served with a white sauce seasoned with Parmesan or nutmeg. Served cold with a mint-flavored vinaigrette (*zucchini a scapece*) or tomato sauce, they can be part of an *antipasto*. They can be halved and stuffed with a meat or vegetable filling. Young zucchini can also be thinly sliced or grated and eaten raw in a salad.

BUYING AND STORING

Zucchini are available almost all year round, but are at their best in spring and summer. The smaller and skinnier zucchini are, the better they taste. They should have very glossy green skins and feel very firm. Do not buy flabby zucchini or those with blemished skins. Larger specimens are useful for stuffing.

Zucchini
These familiar vegetables combine well with other Mediterranean vegetables

Pumpkins
Italians use the flesh of these large vegetables in a multitude of ways

Small pumpkins
Like their larger cousins, these small pumpkins have dense, sweet-tasting flesh

If you can find them in markets, buy tiny zucchini with their flowers attached. Allow 9 oz zucchini per serving. They will keep in the vegetable compartment of the refrigerator for up to a week.

Squashes should feel firm and heavy for their size. It is not worth buying enormous pumpkins (other than for decorative purposes), as their flesh tends to be stringy and flavorless. All whole squashes keep well, but once they are opened, they should be wrapped in plastic wrap and kept in the refrigerator for no more than three days.

If you are lucky enough to find squash or zucchini flowers (the best way is to grow your own), they must be cooked immediately, as they are extremely perishable.

PREPARING ZUCCHINI, SQUASHES AND PUMPKINS

Zucchini should be trimmed, then sliced, diced, cut into batons or grated as appropriate. They do not need peeling.

Flowers may contain small insects, so wash them quickly under cold running water and gently pat dry with paper towels. Cut off all but 1 in of the stems. Zucchini are best sautéed in butter or olive oil flavored with plenty of chopped garlic and parsley. Zucchini deep fried in a light batter are a favorite appetizer or side dish in Italy. The flowers can be prepared in the same way. To make zucchini a scapece, slice 2¼ lb zucchini and brown in hot olive oil. Place in a dish and scatter on about 20 torn mint leaves and 1 finely chopped garlic clove. Season and dress with one part red wine vinegar and two parts olive oil. Mix well and let the flavors develop for 2 hours before serving.

Squashes and pumpkins should be peeled and the seeds and fibrous parts removed. Cut the flesh into chunks or slices. The skin of large pumpkins may be too hard to peel; if so, break open the pumpkin with a hammer or drop it on the floor, and scoop out the flesh, discarding the seeds.

Pumpkin and squash should be blanched in boiling salted water, then sweated in butter until soft and made into soup or stuffing, cooked au gratin or grated raw and added to a risotto. Pumpkin can also be sweetened and used as a pie filling.

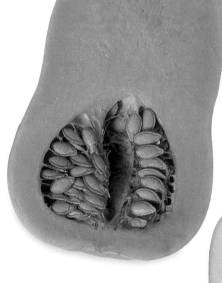

Butternut squash
The brightly colored flesh of butternut squashes is widely used in northern Italian cooking

Acorn squash
Once halved, these small squashes need to be seeded and peeled before cooking

Salad Greens

Italians grow salad greens in profusion and gather them from the wild to create inventive and interesting combinations, such as *misticanza*, a potpourri of wild greens and cultivated leaves. In high season, you will find at least a dozen different salad greens at an Italian market, ranging from fresh green round garden lettuces to bitter dark green grass-like leaves and purplish-red radicchio. Such salads are served after the main course, simply dressed with olive oil and vinegar to cleanse the palate.

Cicoria di campo or dente di leone (dandelion)

Dandelion leaves are rich in iron and vitamins, and are also reputed to be a powerful diuretic. They have a pungent, peppery taste and long, fresh green indented leaves (hence the name "lion's tooth"). They can be picked in the wild before the plant has flowered, but only the young leaves should be eaten. Cultivated dandelion leaves are available. They are more tender than wild leaves, but have a less intense flavor.

CULINARY USES
Young dandelion leaves are usually served raw in salads together with other leaves; they are particularly good with crisply cooked bacon and hard-cooked eggs. They can also be cooked like spinach.

Radicchio

This variety of red-leafed chicory comes originally from Treviso. *Radicchio di Treviso* has elongated purplish-red leaves with pronounced cream-colored veins. The more familiar round variety is known as *radicchio di Verona*. Both types of red-leafed chicory have a bitter taste, and for salads are best used in small quantities together with other leaves. They look particularly attractive when combined with frilly-leafed curly endive, pale whitish-green chicory leaves, or the darker arugula.

Dandelion leaves
Pick these peppery-tasting leaves from the wild before the plant has flowered

Radicchio di Verona
The more familiar round red-leafed chicory

Radicchio di Treviso
This elongated variety is delicious grilled with olive oil

CULINARY USES
Radicchio can also be eaten as a hot vegetable, either quartered and grilled with olive oil, or stuffed with a mixture of bread crumbs, anchovies, capers and olives and baked—but it loses its beautiful color when cooked. A little radicchio added to a risotto made with red wine will add to the pretty pink color.

BUYING AND STORING
Radicchio leaves should be fresh-looking with no trace of brown at the edges. *Radicchio di Verona* should be firm with tightly packed leaves. Both types will keep in the refrigerator for up to a week.

Rucola *(arugula)*

Arugula has dark green elongated, indented leaves and a hot, pungent flavor and aroma. Like dandelions, it grows wild in the Italian countryside, but it is also cultivated

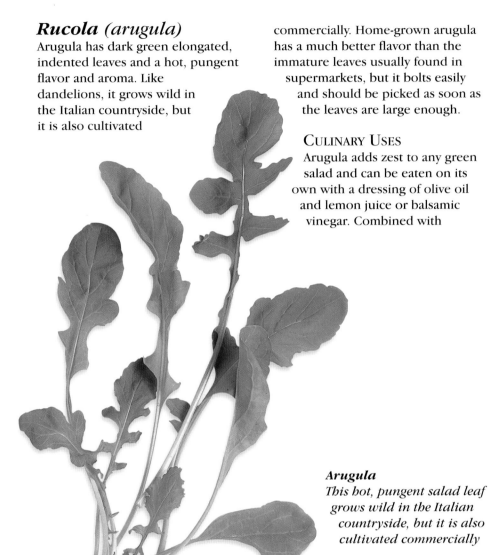

commercially. Home-grown arugula has a much better flavor than the immature leaves usually found in supermarkets, but it bolts easily and should be picked as soon as the leaves are large enough.

CULINARY USES

Arugula adds zest to any green salad and can be eaten on its own with a dressing of olive oil and lemon juice or balsamic vinegar. Combined with

Arugula
This hot, pungent salad leaf grows wild in the Italian countryside, but it is also cultivated commercially

radicchio, lamb's lettuce and fresh herbs, arugula makes a good substitute for *misticanza*. It can be added to pasta sauces and risotto, or cooked like spinach, but cooking does diminish the pungent flavor.

BUYING AND STORING

In Italy, arugula is always sold in small bunches. The leaves should look very fresh with no sign of wilting. Arugula does not keep well unless it has been pre-packaged. To keep it for a day or two, wrap it in damp newspaper or damp paper towels and store in the refrigerator.

Valeriana *(lamb's lettuce)*

This delicate salad plant, called lamb's lettuce, has tender green rounded leaves bunched together in a rosette shape. It grows wild in fields in Italy, but is also cultivated and is an essential ingredient of *misticanza*. It has a delicate but distinctive flavor, which adds interest to winter salads.

CULINARY USES

Lamb's lettuce is usually served by itself or in a mixed green salad, but it can also be cooked like spinach. The tender leaves will blacken if damaged, so take care when tossing a salad not to bruise them.

BUYING AND STORING

Lamb's lettuce should look fresh and green, with no drooping leaves. The smaller and rounder the leaves, the better the flavor. It will keep in the salad compartment of the refrigerator for several days, but take care not to squash it.

Lamb's lettuce
The delicate but distinctive flavor of this salad plant adds interest to winter salads

PREPARING LAMB'S LETTUCE

Lamb's Lettuce is sold with the root attached, so it must be washed before use. Dunk it in several changes of cold water to remove all the grit, then dab the leaves dry with paper towels, handling them very gently.

Mushrooms

Italian country-dwellers have always been passionate collectors of edible wild mushrooms; in spring and autumn, the woods and fields are alive with furtive fungi hunters in search of these flavorful delicacies. Cultivated button mushrooms are rarely eaten in Italy, even when fresh wild varieties are out of season; Italians prefer to use dried or preserved wild fungi with their robust, earthy taste.

The most prized mushroom for use in Italian cooking is the *porcino* (cepe). Since these are extremely expensive, they are most often dried and used in small quantities to add flavor to field or other wild mushrooms. Drying actually intensifies the flavor of *porcini*, so they are not regarded as inferior to the fresh mushrooms—quite the reverse. Other popular wild fungi include *gallinacci* (chanterelles), *prataioli* (field mushrooms) and *ovoli* (Caesar's mushrooms).

HISTORY

From earliest times, man gathered and ate wild mushrooms. The Greeks and Romans enjoyed many fungi, including *amanita caesarea* (Caesar's mushroom), which was popular with the Emperor Claudius and ultimately his downfall; his wife Agrippina poisoned him by adding deadly *amanita phalloides* (the aptly named deathcap) to a dish of his favorite fungi. The Romans succeeded in cultivating several types of mushrooms, but cultivation on a large scale really began in the seventeenth century, when a French botanist discovered how to grow mushrooms in compost all year round.

STORING

Never store mushrooms in a plastic bag, as they will sweat and turn mushy. Put them into a paper bag and keep in the vegetable compartment of the refrigerator for no more than two days.

PREPARING AND COOKING MUSHROOMS

Mushrooms should never be washed or they will become waterlogged and mushy. To clean them, cut off the earthy base of the stalk and lightly brush the caps with a soft brush or wipe them clean with a slightly damp cloth.

With very few exceptions (including cepes and Caesar's mushrooms, which can be eaten raw), wild mushrooms should be cooked to destroy any mild toxins they may contain. All mushrooms can be sliced and sautéed in hot olive oil or a mixture of butter and olive oil with finely chopped garlic or shallots, a little red chili and herbs (parsley, marjoram, thyme or mint are particularly good).

Chanterelles
These orangey-yellow mushrooms have a delicious, delicate flavor and a distinct apricot aroma

COOKING CHANTERELLES

Chanterelles have a delicious, delicate flavor and a slightly chewy texture; they should be cooked slowly or they may become hard. Fry them gently in butter with chopped garlic or shallots for about 10 minutes, adding some finely chopped parsley, marjoram or thyme toward the end of the cooking time. Serve them on hot buttered toast, or add to omelets or scrambled eggs. They are particularly good with poultry, rabbit or veal and can also be dressed with a herb-flavored vinaigrette and served warm in a salad.

Ovoli (Caesar's mushrooms; Latin name amanita caesarea)

These large mushrooms with an orangey-yellow cap have an excellent flavor and were a favorite of the Roman emperors. They are still found in Italy, but are very rare elsewhere.

CULINARY USES

Ovoli can be thinly sliced and eaten raw in a salad. They combine very well with hazelnuts.

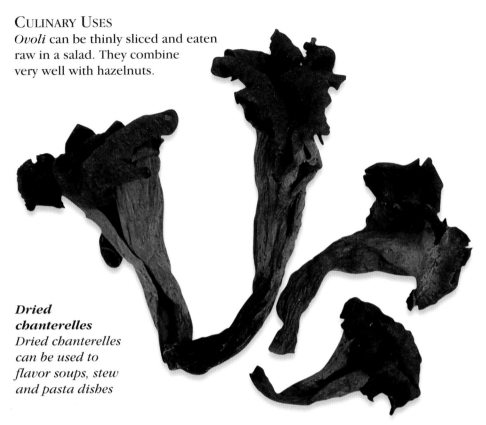

Dried chanterelles
Dried chanterelles can be used to flavor soups, stew and pasta dishes

Mushroom powder

Well-flavored dried mushrooms can be crushed to a powder and used to flavor sauces, soups and stews. Some Italian delicatessens stock mushroom powder. If you make your own, store it in an airtight container.

RECONSTITUTING DRIED MUSHROOMS

Soak 1 oz dried mushrooms in 1 cup hot water for about 20 minutes until soft, then drain and use like fresh mushrooms. Keep the soaking water to use in sauces, stocks or soups; it will have an intense mushroom flavor.

DRYING CHANTERELLES

Leave the chanterelles whole, or halve them if they are large.

Lay them on a double thickness of newspaper and let sit in a very warm, airy place (above the heater is ideal), turning them over every few hours until they have become completely dry and brittle. Alternatively, string them like necklaces and hang them up to dry, or place in a very cool convection oven (maximum 250°F), leaving the door ajar. When the chanterelles are completely dry, store them in jars or paper bags. All mushrooms can be dried in this way; slice them thinly before drying. It is only worth drying perfect specimens.

Mushrooms

Porcini (cepes)

These are the king of mushrooms in Italian cooking. Their Italian name means "little piglets," which aptly describes their bulbous stalks and rounded brown caps. In autumn, they are found in woodlands, where they can grow to an enormous size, weighing more than 1¼ lb each (although mushroom-hunters rarely leave them for long enough to grow to these proportions). There are many different varities of *porcini*, all of which have a fine flavor and meaty texture.

CULINARY USES

All cepes can be cooked in the same way as other mushrooms. Young ones can be thinly sliced and eaten raw, dressed with extra virgin olive oil. Larger caps are delicious brushed with olive oil, grilled and served with a grinding of salt and pepper. Don't discard the stalks, which have an excellent flavor; chop them and cook with the caps, or use them for sauces, stocks and soups; just trim off the earthy bits from the base.

DRYING

Cepes can be thinly sliced and dried in the same way as *gallinacci*. Dried *porcini* are commercially available. They are very expensive, but a little goes a long way. Just 1 oz dried *porcini*, soaked and drained, will enhance the flavor of 1¼ lb cultivated mushrooms beyond recognition. Don't be tempted to buy cheap packages of dried *porcini*, which may contain a high proportion of inferior dried mushrooms and bits of twig from the forest floor.

STORING

Fresh *porcini* can be kept in the vegetable compartment of the refrigerator for up to two days. Dried mushrooms will keep in an airtight container for at least a year.

Porcini *(cepes)*
Italian cooks consider these to be the king of mushrooms

FREEZING

Small *porcini* in perfect condition can be frozen whole. Large or blemished specimens should be sliced and lightly sautéed in butter, then drained and frozen. Do not defrost before use, or they will become mushy. Simply cook the frozen mushrooms in hot olive oil or butter. Frozen mushrooms will only keep for about one month.

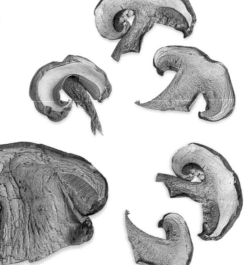

PICKLING *PORCINI*

Unblemished fresh porcini *can be preserved by pickling. Choose unblemished fungi (if you don't have enough* porcini, *use a mixture of mushrooms), leaving small ones whole and slicing or quartering large ones.*
2¼ lb mushrooms
  generous 2 cups white wine
    vinegar
  generous 2 cups water
2 tsp salt
1 tsp peppercorns,
  lightly crushed
2 bay leaves
2 tsp coriander seeds
2 garlic cloves, peeled
  and halved
4 small dried red chilies
olive oil

1 Put the mushrooms in a saucepan with all the ingredients except the olive oil. Bring to a boil and simmer for 5–10 minutes, until the mushrooms are tender but still firm. Drain them, reserving the pickling aromatics, and let cool completely.

2 Spoon the mushrooms and aromatics into a sterilized preserving jar and fill up the jar with olive oil. Seal and let sit for at least a month. Pickled mushrooms will keep for at least six months.

Dried porcini *(cepes)*
These dried porcini *are expensive to buy, but since drying actually accentuates their flavor, a little goes a long way ·*

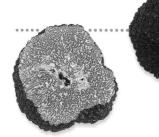

Black truffles
No one has succeeded in cultivating truffles, so they remain rare and expensive—the black variety is more highly prized than the white

White truffles
Found in Piedmont, northern Italy, these delicately flavored truffles are usually served raw

Chiodini *(honey fungus; Latin name armillaria mellea)*

No gardener welcomes the sight of honey fungus (the Italian name means "little nails"), as it is a parasitic fungus that destroys the trees on whose roots it grows. However, the caps of these small golden mushrooms are good to eat (the fibrous stalks should be discarded). In their raw state they are mildly toxic, but once they have been blanched in very hot oil or boiling water, then stewed in butter with a little garlic, seasoning and parsley, they make good eating.

CULINARY USES
Honey fungus makes a good filling for a *frittata* (Italian omelet). Allow 5 oz *chiodini* caps and 4 large eggs for two people. Season the eggs and beat them lightly with 1 oz grated Parmesan. Heat 2 tbsp olive oil in a frying pan and sauté the blanched mushroom caps with 1 chopped garlic clove and 1 tbsp chopped parsley for about 3 minutes. Season with salt and pepper, pour in the eggs and stir well. Cook the *frittata* until set on the bottom, then sprinkle with a little more Parmesan and place under a hot grill until golden brown. Cut into wedges and serve hot or cold.

Tartufi *(truffles)*

Truffles grow 8 in underground, usually near oak trees. They are in season from October to late December. Their irregular, knobby, round shape conceals a pungent, earthy and delicious aroma and flavor. There are two main varieties, black and white. The more highly prized black truffles (*tuber melanosporum*) grow mostly in the Périgord region of France, but they are also found in northern Italy, in Tuscany and Piedmont. The more common Piedmont truffle is the white variety (*tuber magnatum*), which has a more delicate flavor.

No one has yet succeeded in cultivating truffles commercially, so they remain rare and expensive. They are sniffed out by trained pigs or dogs, who can detect their subterranean scent. In order to develop their full aroma and flavor, the truffles must be left to mature, so truffle-hunters often cover up those that the animals have unearthed (praying that nobody else will find their buried treasure) until they reach full maturity.

HISTORY
Truffles have been eaten since ancient times. They were a favorite dish of the ancient Egyptians. The Greeks and Romans believed them to have aphrodisiac properties, but in the Middle Ages they were thought to be manifestations of the devil. Louis XIV of France, however, subscribed to the earlier theory, and from his reign on truffles were enthusiastically consumed by all those rich enough to afford this luxury food.

CULINARY USES
Truffles can be eaten raw or cooked. White Piedmont truffles are usually served raw, shaved very thinly over fresh pasta, a *fonduta* or eggs. They can be heated briefly in butter and seasoned with salt, white pepper and nutmeg. Black or white truffles are delicious with all poultry and white meat. A few slivers of truffle will add a touch of luxury to almost any savory sauce. A classic rich Italian dish using truffles is *vincisgrassi*, sheets of fresh pasta layered with butter, cream, slivers of truffle, ham and chicken livers. It is a speciality of the Marches and the Abruzzi.

BUYING AND STORING
If you are lucky enough to find a fresh truffle, use it as soon as possible, as the flavor is volatile. Brush off the earth from the skin and peel the truffle (keep the peelings to use in a sauce). To give whole fresh eggs the most wonderful flavor, put them in a bowl with the truffle, cover and let sit overnight; they will absorb the superb musty aroma.

You are more likely to buy canned or bottled truffles than fresh. Whole ones are extremely expensive, but cheaper pieces and even peelings are available. The most economical way to enjoy the flavor of truffles is to buy Italian oil scented with white truffles. A drop or two of this added to a dish will transform it into something really special.

Truffle oil
The most economical way to enjoy the flavor of truffles— a drop or two of this scented oil will enhance sauces, pastas and salads

Fruits & Nuts

Italians prefer to buy only those fruits and nuts that are in season, and who can blame them? Italy produces an abundance of berries, pitted fruits and citrus fruits, all bursting with flavor and often available fresh from the tree. There are apples and pears from the orchards of the northern regions; nuts, peaches, plums and figs from the central plains; while the south and Sicily produce almost every kind of fruit—grapes, cherries, oranges and lemons—as well as pistachios and almonds. Many of these fruits are indigenous to Italy and have been grown there since time immemorial.

After a full meal of *antipasto*, pasta and a *secondo* (main course), it is hardly surprising that Italian desserts very often consist of nothing but a bowl of seasonal fresh fruit served on its own or made into a refreshing *macedonia* (fruit salad). Berries form the basis of ice creams, sorbets, *granite* and *frullati* (fresh fruit milkshakes), while nuts and winter fruits (often dried or candied) are baked into tarts and pastries.

Amarena (Morello cherry)

Although Italy does produce sweet dessert cherries, it is best known for the bitter Morello variety, which are preserved in syrup or brandy, or made into ice cream and Maraschino liqueur. These cherries are small, with dark red skins and firm flesh. They are in season from late June to early July, and can be eaten raw, although they have quite a sharp flavor.

CULINARY USES

Morello cherries can be poached in sugar syrup and served whole, or puréed and made into a rich, dark, cherry syrup. Pit the cherries and purée them. Strain the cherries through a fine sieve and let the juice sit at room temperature for about 24 hours. Strain through muslin and add 1 lb, 10 oz sugar per generous 2 cups cherry juice. Heat gently. When the sugar has dissolved, bring the cherry syrup to a boil, strain again and pour into airtight bottles or containers. These cherries also

make excellent jam. A popular Venetian dish is Morello cherries poached in a red wine syrup flavored with cinnamon. Bottled cherries in vinegar can be used in sauces for meat, duck and game.

BUYING AND STORING

Choose fresh cherries with unwrinkled and unblemished skins, which look shiny and feel firm. Stored in a plastic bag, they will keep in the refrigerator for up to a week.

Morello cherries
These dark red cherries are usually preserved in syrup and used for desserts. Those bottled in vinegar can be used for savory recipes

Arancia (orange)

Many varieties of oranges are grown in Sicily and southern Italy. The best-known Sicilian oranges are the small blood oranges with their bright ruby-red flesh. Other types of sweet oranges include seedless navels, which take their name from the umbilical-like end which contains an embryonic orange, and seeded late oranges, which have paler flesh and are available throughout the winter. Bitter oranges (*arance amare*) are also grown; these rough-skinned varieties are made into preserves (although rarely marmalade in Italy), candied peel and *liquore all'arancia* (orange liqueur).

HISTORY

Oranges originated in China, but bitter oranges may possibly have been known in Ancient Greece; the mythical "golden apples of the Hesperides" are said by some to have been Seville oranges, although this seems historically far-fetched. They were certainly brought to Italy by Arab traders during the Roman Empire and over the centuries became a symbol of wealth and opulence—so much so that the Medici family incorporated them into their coat of arms as five golden balls. Sweet oranges did not arrive in Italy until the seventeenth century.

Oranges
Sweet varieties are used for both sweet and savory recipes—they are a favorite addition to salads

Bitter oranges
This rough-skinned variety can be used to add zest to savory dishes—it combines well with white fish, liver, duck and game—and is used for preserves

CULINARY USES

A favorite Sicilian recipe is *insalata di arance alla siciliana*, a salad of thinly sliced oranges and red onion rings dressed with black olives and their oil. Oranges also combine well with raw fennel and chicory. They can be sliced and served *alla veneziana*, coated with caramel, or simply macerated in a little lemon juice with a sliver of lemon peel for a refreshing dessert. They can be squeezed for juice, or made into sorbet and *granita*. Bitter oranges combine well with white fish, calf's liver, duck or game, and add zest to a tomato sauce.

BUYING AND STORING

Oranges are available all year round, but are at their best in winter. They should have unblemished shiny skins and feel heavy for their size (this indicates that they contain plenty of juice and that the flesh is not dry). If you intend to candy the peel or incorporate it into a recipe, choose unwaxed oranges. Oranges will keep at room temperature for a week and for at least two weeks in the refrigerator. Bring them back to room temperature or warm them slightly before eating them.

Preparing Fresh Oranges

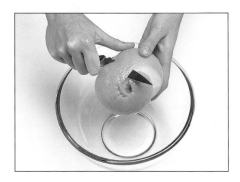

1 When peeling an orange it is important to remove all the bitter white pith and membrane. Hold the orange over a bowl to catch the juice and use a very sharp knife to cut off the peel, pith and the membrane enclosing the flesh.

2 To segment the orange, cut down between the membranes of the segments and ease out the flesh. Squeeze the membranes into the bowl to extract the juice.

3 To remove strips of orange rind, run a paring knife down the orange, or use a zester for finer shreds. If you cannot find unwaxed fruit, wash the oranges in warm water, rinse and dry well before removing strips of rind.

Fruit

Fico (fig)

Figs are grown all over Italy, but thanks to the hot climate Sicilian figs are perhaps the most luscious of all. During the summer months you will often find Italian farmers at the roadside selling containers of ripe figs from their own trees. There are two types of Italian figs, green and purple. Both have thin, tender skins and very sweet, succulent, red flesh, and are rich in Vitamins A, B and C. They are in season from July to October and are best eaten straight off the tree when they are perfectly ripe.

Purple figs
The sweet succulent flesh of this variety makes a perfect partner to nuts of all kinds

HISTORY

Figs were said to grow in the Garden of Eden, where Adam and Eve used the leaves to cover their nakedness. In fact they probably originated in Asia Minor, although the oldest fig tree in the world is reputed to be growing in a garden in Palermo in Sicily. The Greeks and Romans certainly enjoyed figs, which are still as highly prized today.

CULINARY USES

Fresh figs are delicious served on their own, but they have an affinity with nuts such as walnuts, pistachios and almonds. They can be served raw with prosciutto or salami as an *antipasto*, or stuffed with raspberry coulis or mascarpone as a dessert. Poached in a little water or wine flavored with cinnamon or nutmeg, they make an excellent accompaniment to duck, game or lamb.

BUYING AND STORING

Ripe figs are extremely delicate and do not travel well, so it is hard to find imported fruit at a perfect stage of maturity. In season in Italy, however, you can find local figs that are just ripe for eating; they should be soft and yielding, but not squashy. Sometimes the skin may have split, revealing the luscious red or pink flesh. As long as you are going to eat the fig immediately, this does not matter. Take great care not to squash the figs on your way home, or you will end up with a squishy, inedible mess.

Under-ripe figs can be kept at room temperature for a day or two until the skin softens, but they will never develop the fine flavor of tree-ripened figs. Ripe figs should be eaten on the day they are bought.

Green figs
Delicious served raw with prosciutto or salami as an antipasto

PREPARING AND COOKING FIGS

Wash the figs briefly and gently pat dry. Discard the stalk and peel the figs, if desired.

To serve as an antipasto *or dessert, cut them downward from the stalk end into quarters, leaving them attached at the base. Open them out like flowers.*

Perfectly ripe figs are best eaten raw, but less perfect specimens can be improved by cooking. They can be gently poached in syrup or red wine flavored with a cinnamon stick or vanilla pod, or rolled in sugar and baked in the oven until caramelized. Barely ripe figs also make excellent jam.

Limone (lemon)

Lemons are grown all over Italy, even in the northern regions. Lake Garda even boasts a town called Limone, named for its abundance of lemon trees. But the most famous Italian lemons come from the Amalfi coast, where they grow to an extraordinary size and have such a sweet flavor that they can almost be eaten as a dessert fruit. Their aromatic flavor enhances almost any dish, and they have the added advantage of being rich in Vitamin C.

HISTORY

Lemons originated in India or Malaysia and were brought by the Assyrians to Greece, which in turn took them to Italy. The Greeks and Romans greatly appreciated their culinary and medicinal qualities. Later seafarers ate them in large quantities to protect against scurvy, and society ladies used them as a beauty treatment to whiten their skin, bleach their hair and redden their lips.

CULINARY USES

Lemons are extraordinarily versatile. The juice can be squeezed to make a refreshing *spremuta di limone*, or it can be added to other cold drinks or tea. It is an antioxidant, which prevents discoloration when applied to other fruits and vegetables. The juice is used for dressings and for flavoring all sorts of drinks and sauces. A squeeze of lemon juice adds a different dimension to intrinsically bland foods, such as fish, poultry, veal or certain vegetables. Its acidity also helps to bring out the flavor of other fruits. The zest makes a wonderfully aromatic flavoring for cakes and pastries, and is an essential ingredient of *gremolata*, a topping of grated zest, garlic and parsley for *osso buco*. Quartered lemons are always served with *fritto misto di mare* (mixed fried fish) and other foods fried in batter.

PREPARING LEMONS

Before squeezing a lemon, warm it gently: Either put it in a bowl, pour boiling water over the top and let stand for about 5 minutes or, if you prefer, microwave the lemon on full power for about 30 seconds—this will significantly increase the quantity of juice you will obtain.

For sweet dishes, when you want to add the flavor of lemons, but not the grated rind, rub a sugar lump over the skin of the lemon to absorb the oil, then use the sugar as part of the recipe.

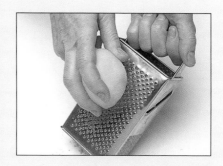

To prepare grated lemon rind, thoroughly wash and dry unwaxed lemons. Grate the rind or peel it off with a zester, taking care not to include any white pith.

BUYING AND STORING

Depending on the variety, lemons may have thick indented skin, or be perfectly smooth. Their appearance does not affect the flavor, but they should feel heavy for their size. If you intend to use the zest, buy unwaxed lemons. Lemons will keep in the refrigerator for up to two weeks.

Lemons
Lemons are grown all over Italy— their aromatic flavor enhances almost any dish

Fruits

Melone (melon)

Many different varieties of sweet, aromatic melons are grown in Italy, and each has its own regional name. *Napoletano* melons have a smooth pale green rind and delicately scented orange flesh. *Cantalupo* (cantaloupe) melons have a warty skin, which is conveniently marked into segments, and highly scented deep yellow flesh. A similar Tuscan melon with gray-green rind and orange flesh is called *popone*. These melons are all perfect for eating with Prosciutto or salami as an *antipasto*.

Watermelons (*anguria* or *cocomero*) are grown in Tuscany. These huge green melons with their refreshing bright pink or red flesh and edible brown seeds can be round or sausage-shaped. In Florence, the feast of San Lorenzo, the patron saint of cooks, is celebrated with an orgy of watermelons on August 10th. During this season, roadside stalls groan under the weight of hundreds of these gigantic fruits.

CULINARY USES

Italians eat melon as an appetizer, usually accompanied by wafer-thin *prosciutto crudo* or cured meats. Melons and watermelons are occasionally served as a dessert fruit on their own, but more often appear in a *macedonia* (fruit salad).

BUYING AND STORING

The best way to tell whether a melon is ripe is to smell it; it should have a mild, sweet scent. If it smells highly perfumed and musky, it will be over-ripe. The fruit should feel heavy for its size and the skin should not be bruised or damaged. Gently press the rind with your thumbs at the stalk end; it should give a little. Melons will ripen quickly at room temperature and should be eaten within two or three days. Wrap cut melon tightly in plastic wrap before storing in the refrigerator, or its scent may permeate other foods.

PREPARING MELON

For serving as an antipasto, *cut the melon into wedges, scoop out the seeds and run a flexible knife between the rind and flesh. Remove the rind before serving.*

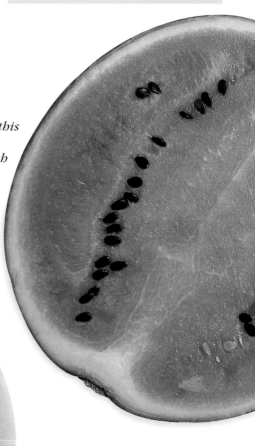

Napoletano melon
The sweet scented flesh of this and the similar cantaloupe melon is perfect for eating with prosciutto as an antipasto

Pesche (peaches) *and* pesche noci *(nectarines)*

Peaches, with their velvety skin and sweet, juicy flesh, are a summer fruit grown in central and southern Italy. The most common variety is the *pesca gialla* (yellow peach), which has succulent, yellow flesh. More highly prized are the *pesche bianche* (white peaches), whose pink-tinted flesh is full of juice and flavor.

Nectarines have smooth plum-like skins and taste very similar to peaches. They also come in yellow and white varieties and, like peaches, the white nectarines have a finer flavor. Some people prefer nectarines as a dessert fruit because they do not require peeling. Peaches and nectarines are interchangeable in cooked dishes.

CULINARY USES

Peaches and nectarines are delicious served as a dessert fruit, but can also be macerated in fortified wine or spirits or poached in white wine and syrup. They have a particular affinity with almonds; a favorite Italian dessert is *pesche ripiene alla piemontese*, halved peaches stuffed with crumbled almond-flavored amaretti cookies and baked in white wine. They are also delicious served with raspberries, or made into fruit drinks (the famous Bellini cocktail is made with fresh peach juice) and ice creams and sorbets.

BUYING AND STORING

Peaches are in season from June to September. Make sure they are ripe, but not too soft, with unwrinkled and unblemished skins. They should have a sweet, intense scent. Peaches and nectarines bruise very easily, so try to buy those that have been kept in compartmented trays rather than piled into crates.

Do not keep peaches and nectarines for more than a day or two. If they are very ripe, store them in the refrigerator; underripe fruit will ripen in a couple of days if kept in a brown paper bag at room temperature.

PREPARING PEACHES

To peel peaches, place them in a heatproof bowl and pour boiling water over them. Let sit for 15–30 seconds (depending on how ripe they are), then refresh in very cold water; the skins will slip off easily.

Peaches
This summer fruit is grown in central and southern Italy

Watermelon
Occasionally served on its own in wedges as a dessert, this vibrant red fruit is more usually chopped and added to a fruit salad

Nectarines
These smooth-skinned fruits are delicious served as a dessert fruit

Fruits

Uva (grapes)

Italy is the world's largest producer of grapes of all kinds. Almost every rural property boasts an expanse of vineyards, some producing wine-making grapes intended only for home consumption. Others (particularly in Chianti and the south) are destined for the enormous Italian wine-making industry. But Apulia, Abruzzo and Sicily produce sweet dessert grapes on a vast commercial scale, from large luscious Italia, with their fine muscat flavor, to Cardinal, named for its deep red color, purple Alphonse Lavallé, and various small seedless varieties.

Despite their high caloric value, grapes are extremely good for you, since they are rich in potassium, iron and vitamins.

HISTORY

Wild grapes grew in the Caucasus as early as the Stone Age, and early man soon discovered the secret of cultivating vineyards and making wine. The Greeks and Romans discovered that drying grapes transformed them into sweet raisins. The Gauls invented the wooden wine cask, and from that time on wine production became a major industry.

CULINARY USES

Dessert grapes are best eaten on their own or as an accompaniment to cheese, but they can be used in pastries or as a garnish for cooked quails, guinea fowl or other poultry. The seeds are pressed into grapeseed oil, which has a neutral taste and is high in polyunsaturated fatty acids.

BUYING AND STORING

Choosing white, black or red grapes is a matter of preference; beneath the skin, the flesh is always pale green and juicy. Buy bunches of grapes with fruit which is of equal size and not too densely packed on the stalk. Check that none is withered or rotten. The skin should have a delicate bloom and be firm to the touch. Try to eat one grape from a bunch to see how they taste. The flesh should be firm and very juicy and refreshing.

Grapes should be washed immediately after purchase, then placed in a bowl and kept in the refrigerator for up to three days. Keeping them in a plastic bag causes them to become overripe very quickly.

PREPARING GRAPES

Grapes used for cooking should be peeled and deseeded. Put them in a bowl, pour in boiling water and let sit for 10–20 seconds, depending on the ripeness of the grapes. Peel off the skin. To remove the seeds, halve the grapes and scoop out the seeds with the tip of a pointed knife.

Italia grapes
These luscious red and white grapes have a wonderful Muscat flavor

Nuts

Many different kinds of nuts are grown in Italy—chestnuts and hazelnuts in the north, pine nuts in the coastal regions, and almonds, pistachios and walnuts in the south. They are used in a wide variety of savory dishes, cakes and pastries, or served as a dessert with a glass of *vin santo* (sweet white wine).

Castagne (chestnuts)

These are a mainstay of Tuscan and Sardinian cooking, dating back to the days when the peasants could not afford wheat to make flour, so they ground up the chestnuts that grow in abundance throughout the region instead. Most varieties of sweet chestnut contain two or three

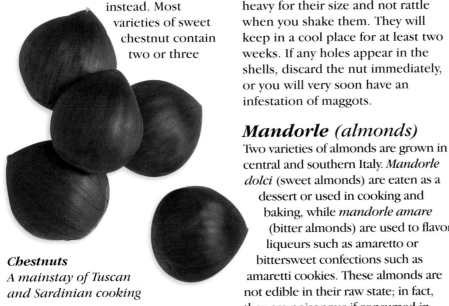

Chestnuts
A mainstay of Tuscan and Sardinian cooking

separate nuts inside the spiky green husk, but commercially grown varieties contain a single, large nut, which is easier to peel and better for serving whole.

Chestnuts have shiny, rich reddish-brown shells with a wrinkled, thin skin beneath, which can be very hard to remove. They cannot be eaten raw, but once cooked, the starchy nuts are highly nutritious and very sustaining.

CULINARY USES
Chestnuts roasted over an open fire conjure up the spirit of autumn. Peeled chestnuts can be boiled, poached in red wine or milk or fried in butter as a garnish. They make hearty soups, or can be puréed into

sauces for game. In Piedmont, they are candied to make *marrons glacés*, and a favorite Italian dessert is *monte bianco*, a rich concoction of puréed chestnuts and cream.

Chestnut flour is still widely used in Tuscany and Liguria, where it is baked into cakes and pastries, such as *castagnaccio*, a confection with pine nuts and herbs.

BUYING AND STORING
The nicest chestnuts are those you gather yourself, but if you are buying them, look for large, shiny specimens, with no tiny holes in the shells. The chestnuts should feel heavy for their size and not rattle when you shake them. They will keep in a cool place for at least two weeks. If any holes appear in the shells, discard the nut immediately, or you will very soon have an infestation of maggots.

Mandorle (almonds)

Two varieties of almonds are grown in central and southern Italy. *Mandorle dolci* (sweet almonds) are eaten as a dessert or used in cooking and baking, while *mandorle amare* (bitter almonds) are used to flavor liqueurs such as amaretto or bittersweet confections such as amaretti cookies. These almonds are not edible in their raw state; in fact, they are poisonous if consumed in large quantities. Both types of almonds have a velvety pale green outer casing; the hard light brown shell within encloses one or two oval nuts.

CULINARY USES
Early in the season (late May), sweet almonds can be eaten raw as a dessert. They have a delicious fresh flavor and the brown skin is still soft enough to be palatable. Later, dried sweet almonds are blanched, slivered or ground to be used for cakes, pastries and all sorts of confectionery, including *marzapane* (marzipan) and *croccante* (almond brittle). They can be devilled or salted as an appetizing

PREPARING CHESTNUTS

There are three possible ways to peel chestnuts.

Slit the domed side of the shells with a very sharp knife, then drop them into boiling water for 5 minutes, or put them in a roasting pan with a little hot water and cook in a very hot oven for about 10 minutes. Shell and skin the chestnuts as soon as they are cool enough to handle. Alternatively, shell the raw chestnuts and boil them in their skins for about 20 minutes, then peel off the skins.

snack with an *aperitivo*. Toasted almonds are the classic garnish for trout, and go well with chicken or rabbit. Dried bitter almonds are used in small quantities to add a more intense flavor to cookies and cakes.

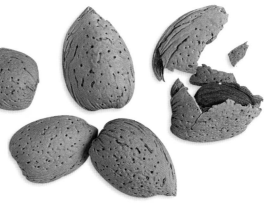

Almonds
In Italy in late spring, fresh almonds are eaten raw as a dessert

Nuts

BUYING AND STORING

Fresh almonds in the shell are available from láte May to late June. They are difficult to crack, so you may prefer to buy shelled nuts. They should look plump, and the skins should not feel too dry. Pre-blanched almonds can often be a disappointment; buy the nuts with their skins on and blanch them yourself. Store shelled almonds in an airtight container for no longer than a month.

Nocciole (hazelnuts)

Fresh hazelnuts are harvested in August and September and during these months are always sold in their frilled green husks. The small round nuts have a very sweet flavor and a milky texture when fresh. In Italy, they are generally dried and used in candy and cakes.

CULINARY USES

Hazelnuts are used in all sorts of confectionery, including *torrone* (a sort of nougat) and *gianduiotti*, a delicious fondant chocolate from Piedmont. The famous chocolate *baci* ("kisses") from Perugia contain a whole hazelnut in the center. Hazelnuts are finely ground to make cakes and cookies, and are excellent in stuffings for poultry and game.

BUYING AND STORING

If hazelnuts are sold in their fresh green husks, you can be sure they are fresh and juicy. Otherwise, look for shiny unblemished shells that are not too thick; cracked shells will cause the nut to shrivel and dry out. Shelled hazelnuts should be kept in an airtight container for no longer than one month.

Hazelnuts
When fresh, these small nuts have a very sweet flavor

Shelled almonds
These dried almonds are used for cakes, pastries and candies

Shelled hazelnuts
These dried nuts are used for candies and cakes

Noci (walnuts)

Walnuts grow in abundance throughout central and southern Italy. The kernels, shaped like the two halves of a brain, grow inside a pale brown, heavily indented shell enclosed by a smooth green fleshy husk or "shuck." Fresh walnuts have a delicious milky sweetness and a soft texture, which hardens as the nuts mature. Walnuts do not need to be skinned before eating.

Walnuts
In Italy, fresh walnuts are very often eaten straight from the shell as a dessert

PREPARING ALMONDS

To blanch almonds, place them in a strainer and plunge into boiling water for a few seconds. As soon as the skin begins to loosen, transfer the almonds to a bowl of cold water and slip off the skins. Dry thoroughly before storing.

CULINARY USES

Fresh walnuts are usually eaten straight from the shell as a dessert. They can be ground or chopped and used in cakes and desserts, or halved and used for decoration. They are used to make savory sauces for pasta, such as *salsa di noci*, a rich combination of ground walnuts, butter and cream. Walnut oil has a distinctive flavor and, used sparingly, makes an excellent salad dressing. Unripe walnuts can be pickled, and they are used to make sweet, sticky liqueurs.

BUYING AND STORING

Fresh "wet" walnuts are available from late September to late October. They should be kept in a wicker basket and eaten within a week. Dried walnuts should not have cracked or broken shells. They will keep for at least two months. Never store walnuts in the refrigerator, as the oil they contain will harden and ruin the flavor. Dried walnut kernels will have the flavor and texture of fresh nuts if they are soaked in milk for at least 4 hours.

Pine nuts
The oily, slightly resinous flavor is accentuated by toasting

Pinoli (pine nuts)

Pine nuts (more accurately known as pine kernels) are actually the seeds from the stone pine trees that grow in profusion along the Adriatic and Mediterranean coasts of Italy. The small, oblong, cream-colored seeds grow inside a hard husk and are extracted from between the scales of the pine cones. The soft-textured kernels, which have an oily, slightly resinous flavor, are always sold de-husked. They can be eaten raw, but are usually toasted before use to bring out the flavor.

CULINARY USES

Pine nuts are used in many Italian dishes, both sweet and savory, but they are best known as an essential ingredient of pesto. They go well with meat and game, and make exceptionally delicious cookies and tarts.

Pistachio nuts
Grown in southern Italy, these sweet, delicately flavored nuts are used in mortadella

PREPARING PINE NUTS

For most recipes and when used as a garnish, they should be lightly toasted. Heat a dry, heavy frying pan, put in the pine nuts and toss quickly until they turn pale golden. Do not let them brown, or they will taste unpleasant.

BUYING AND STORING

Pine nuts are always sold out of the husk. Because they are very oily, they go rancid quite quickly, so buy only as much as you need at any one time. Store them in an airtight container in the fridge for not more than a week.

Pistacchi (pistachios)

Pistachios are native to the Near East, but are grown in southern Italy, particularly Sicily. The small, bright green nut has a yellowish-red skin and is enclosed in a smooth, pale shell. Pistachios have a sweet, delicate flavor, which makes them ideal for desserts, but they are also used to stud mortadella and other pale cooked meat products.

CULINARY USES

Pistachios can be eaten raw or roasted and salted as a snack with an *aperitivo*. Their color enhances most white meats and poultry. They make deliciously rich ice cream and are used in *cassata gelata*, the famous Sicilian dessert.

BUYING AND STORING

If possible, buy pistachios still in their shells. These will be easier to open if they are already slightly ajar; once open, the nut is very easy to remove. Shelled, blanched pistachios are also available. They are useful for cooking, but lack the fine flavor of whole nuts. Store blanched pistachios in an airtight container for up to two weeks. Whole nuts will keep for well over a month.

Herbs & Seasonings

Herbs are vital to Italian cooking. Their aromatic flavor adds depth and interest to what is essentially plain cooking, based on fine, fresh ingredients. It is impossible to imagine roast chicken or veal without rosemary or sage, or tomatoes or pesto without basil. Many wild herbs grow in the Italian countryside, and these are often incorporated into Italian recipes. One of the most popular is mentuccia, *a wild mint with tiny leaves and the delicate favor of marjoram. If a recipe specifies* mentuccia *or its close relative* nepitella, *substitute a smaller quantity of mint.*

Always use fresh herbs whenever you can; the dried varieties have a stronger and often quite different taste, and lack the subtlety of fresh herbs. If you must use dried herbs, try to buy them freeze-dried; these taste much closer to the real thing. As a general rule, you will need only about one-third as much dried herb as fresh—in other words, allow about 1 tsp dried herbs for every 1 tbsp fresh.

Basilico (basil)

Basil, with its intense aroma and fresh, pungently sweet flavor, is associated with Italian cooking more than any other herb. It is an essential ingredient of pesto, but it also finds its way into soups, salads and almost all dishes based on tomatoes, with which it has an extraordinary affinity. There are over 50 varieties of this annual herb, but the one most commonly used in Italy is sweet basil, with its fresh broad green leaves and wonderfully spicy aroma.

CULINARY USES

Basil has a volatile flavor, so it is best added to dishes at the end of cooking. It can be used in any dish that contains tomatoes and is delicious sprinkled on a pizza. It adds a pungent, sweet note to almost all salads and is particularly good with white fish and seafood. It makes an excellent flavoring for omelets and is often added to minestrone. The most famous of all basil dishes is pesto, the fragrant Genovese sauce made by pounding together fresh basil, garlic, Parmesan, pine nuts and olive oil.

BUYING AND STORING

In sunny climates, such as southern Italy, basil grows outdoors all through the summer. In other places it is available cut or growing in pots all year round, so there really is no reason to use dried basil. Look for sweet basil with bright green leaves— the larger the better. If you have grown your own and have a glut, you can freeze basil leaves to preserve the flavor, but they lose their fresh texture and darken in color. Alternatively, put a bunch of basil in a jar and fill up with olive oil for a fragrant flavored oil for dressings. To store fresh cut basil, wrap it in damp paper towels and keep in the vegetable compartment of the refrigerator for up to two days.

Basil
More than any other, this pungent, intensely flavored herb is associated with Italian cooking—it is an essential ingredient in many dishes, including pesto

PREPARING BASIL

Basil leaves are tender and bruise easily, so never chop them with a knife, but tear them lightly with your fingers immediately before using.

Pesto

To make enough pesto for 4–6 servings of pasta, put 2 cups basil leaves in a mortar with ½ cup pine nuts, 2 fat peeled garlic cloves and a large pinch of coarse salt, and crush to a paste with a pestle. Work in ½ cup freshly grated Parmesan. Gradually add about ½ cup extra virgin olive oil, working it in thoroughly with a wooden spoon to make a thick, creamy sauce. Put the pesto in a screwtop jar; it will keep for several weeks in the refrigerator.

Maggiorana (sweet marjoram) and origano (oregano)

These two highly aromatic herbs are closely related (oregano is the wild variety), but marjoram has a much milder flavor. Marjoram is more commonly used in northern Italy, while oregano is widely used in the south to flavor tomato dishes, vegetables and pizzas. Drying greatly intensifies the flavor of both herbs, so they should be used very sparingly.

CULINARY USES

In northern Italy, sweet marjoram is used to flavor meat, poultry, vegetables and soups; the flavor goes particularly well with carrots and cucumber. Despite its rather pungent aroma, marjoram has a delicate flavor, so it should be added to long-cooked foods toward the end of cooking.

Oregano is used exclusively in southern Italian cooking, especially in tomato-based dishes. It is a classic flavoring for pizza, but should always be used in moderation.

BUYING AND STORING

Marjoram and oregano are in season throughout the summer, but cut fresh herbs are available all year round at supermarkets. The leaves dry out quickly, so store them in plastic bags in the refrigerator; they will keep for up to a week. Dried oregano should be stored in small airtight jars away from the light. It loses its pungent flavor after a few months, so only buy a little at a time.

Oregano
Widely used in the south of Italy to flavor tomato dishes

Prezzemolo (parsley)

Italian parsley is the flat leaf variety, which has a more robust flavor than curly parsley. It has attractive dark green leaves, which resemble cilantro. It is used as a flavoring in innumerable cooked dishes, but rarely as a garnish. If flat leaf parsley is not available, curly parsley makes a perfectly adequate substitute. Parsley is an extremely nutritious herb, rich in iron and potassium and Vitamin C.

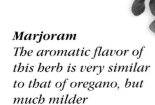

Marjoram
The aromatic flavor of this herb is very similar to that of oregano, but much milder

Parsley
Italian parsley is the flat leafed variety. It has a strong, robust flavor

Herbs & Seasonings

CULINARY USES

Parsley can be used to flavor innumerable savory dishes. It adds color and flavor to sauces, soups and risotto. The stalks can be used to flavor stocks and stews. Chopped parsley can be sprinkled over cooked savory dishes; whole leaves are rarely used as a garnish in Italy.

BUYING AND STORING

Parsley is available all year round, so it should never be necessary to use the dried variety. A large bunch of parsley will keep for up to a week in the fridge if washed and wrapped in damp paper towels. Chopped parsley freezes very well and can be added to cooked dishes straight from the freezer.

Rosmarino (rosemary)

Spiky evergreen rosemary bushes, with their attractive blue flowers, grow wild all over Italy. The herb has a delicious, highly aromatic flavor, which is intensifed when it is dried. The texture of rosemary leaves is quite hard and the flavor very pungent, so it is never used raw, but only in cooking. It can easily overpower a dish, so only a few leaves should be used in a dish.

CULINARY USES

Rosemary combines extremely well with roast or grilled lamb, veal and chicken. A few needles will enhance the flavor of baked fish or any tomato dish, and it adds a wonderful flavor to roast potatoes and onions. Some rosemary branches added to the charcoal on a barbecue impart a superb flavor to whatever is being cooked. Dried rosemary can always be substituted for fresh; it is extremely pungent, so should be used very sparingly.

Salvia (sage)

Wild sage grows in profusion in the Italian countryside. There are several varieties, including the common garden sage, with furry silvery-gray leaves and spiky purple flowers, and clary sage, with hairy curly leaves, which is used to make dry vermouth. All sages have a slightly bitter aromatic flavor, which contrasts well with fatty meats such as pork. In northern Italy, particularly Tuscany, it is used to flavor veal and chicken. It is an excellent medicinal herb (the Latin name means "good health"); an infusion of sage leaves makes a good gargle for a sore throat.

CULINARY USES

Used sparingly, sage combines well with almost all meat and vegetable dishes and is often used in minestrone. It has a particular affinity with veal (such as *osso buco*, *piccata* and, of course, calf's

Sage
Several varieties of this herb grow in profusion in the Italian countryside

liver) and is an essential ingredient of *saltimbocca alla romana*, veal scallops and *prosciutto crudo* topped with sage leaves and sautéed in butter and white wine. In Tuscany, white beans (*fagioli*) are often flavored with sage.

BUYING AND STORING

Fresh sage is very easy to grow on a sunny windowsill. It is available in both fresh and dried forms at supermarkets all year round. Dried sage is very strongly flavored, so should be used in tiny quantities. It starts to taste musty after a few weeks, so replace it fairly frequently. Fresh sage should be stored in a plastic bag in the refrigerator; it will keep for up to a week.

Rosemary
The highly aromatic flavor of this herb is intensified when it is dried

Aceto *(vinegar)*

Like all wine-making countries, Italy produces excellent red and white wine vinegar as a byproduct. The best vinegar is made from good wines, which are fermented in oak casks to give a depth of flavor. Good vinegar should be clean-tasting and aromatic, with no trace of bitterness, and it should be transparent, not cloudy. White wine vinegar is pale golden with a pinkish tinge; red wine vinegar ranges from deep pink to dark red.

Aceto balsamico *(balsamic vinegar)*

Balsamic vinegar is the king of vinegars. Its name means "balm-like," reflecting its digestive qualities. Indeed, the best has a flavor so mellow and sweet that it can be drunk on its own as a *digestivo*. Balsamic vinegar is made in the area around Modena; the boiled and concentrated juice of local *trebbiano* grapes is aged in a series of barrels of decreasing size and different woods over a long period— sometimes as long as 50 years —which gives it a slightly syrupy texture and a rich, deep mahogany color. Like Parmigiano Reggiano and prosciutto, genuine balsamic vinegar (*aceto balsamico tradizionale di Modena)* is strictly controlled by law; it must have been aged in the wood for at least 12 years. Vinegar aged 20 years or more is called *stravecchio.*

CULINARY USES

Red and white wine vinegars are principally used to make salad dressings and marinades, or to preserve vegetables *sott'aceto* for *antipasti*. They also add the requisite sharpness to sauces such as *agrodolce* (sweet-and-sour). Good balsamic vinegar is also used as a dressing, sometimes on its own. It can be used to finish a delicate sauce for white fish, poultry or calf's liver. A few drops sprinkled over ripe strawberries will enhance their flavor.

BUYING AND STORING

Price is usually an indication of quality where vinegar is concerned, so always buy the best you can afford. Genuine balsamic vinegar must be labeled *aceto balsamico tradizionale di Modena*; products that purport to be the real thing but are not labeled as such have either not been aged for long enough or, worse, are just red wine vinegar colored and flavored with caramel. Proper balsamic vinegar is expensive, but the flavor is so concentrated that a little goes a long way, and it is worth paying more for the genuine article. Vinegar will keep in a cool dark place for many months.

Balsamic vinegar
This is the king of vinegars and has a wonderfully sweet and mellow flavor

Red and white wine vinegars
These vinegars have a sharp flavor and are used primarily for salad dressings

Herbs & Seasonings

Aglio (garlic)

Garlic is not, as you might suppose, a type of onion, but is a member of the lily family. The bulb or "head" is a collection of cloves held together by a papery white or purplish skin. When crushed or chopped it releases a pungent, slightly acrid oil with a very distinctive flavor and smell. Freshly picked garlic is milder than older, dried garlic, and the large, mauve-tinged variety has a more delicate flavor than the smaller white variety.

Garlic finds its way into many Italian dishes, but it is generally used with discretion so as not to flavor the food too aggressively. It is indispensable to certain dishes such as *bagna cauda* (hot anchovy and garlic dip), *spaghetti all'aglio e olio* (garlic and olive oil) and pesto. In the south, garlic is used to flavor tomato sauces and fish soups.

CULINARY USES

Used in small quantities, garlic enlivens almost any sauce, soup or stew. It can be roasted with lamb and potatoes, or baked in its skin for a mellower flavor. Blanched, crushed garlic will aromatize olive oil to make an excellent dressing for salads or to use in cooking where only a hint of garlic flavor is required. Raw, skinned garlic cloves can be rubbed over toasted croutons to make flavorful *bruschetta* bases.

BUYING AND STORING

Garlic sold loose by the head is usually fresher and better than pre-packaged varieties. The heads should feel firm and the skin should not be too papery. Do not buy garlic that is sprouting green shoots; the cloves will be soft and of no culinary value.

Stored in a cool dry place, garlic will keep for many months. If possible, hang the heads in bunches to keep them aerated. Once garlic has become soft or withered, it is useless, so throw it away.

Garlic
Italian cooks prefer to use garlic with discretion, but it is indispensable to many dishes. The purple-skinned variety has a more delicate flavor than the white variety

PREPARING AND COOKING GARLIC

To peel garlic, cut off the root end with a small sharp knife and peel the skin upward.

Alternatively, lay a garlic clove on the work surface, place the flat side of a heavy knife blade on top and bring the side of your fist sharply down on to the blade. This will flatten the garlic and split the skin.

To chop garlic, halve the clove and remove the bitter-tasting green shoot. Chop the garlic as finely as possible.

For very fine garlic, crush it in a garlic press.

Garlic should be softened gently in oil or butter; it will become very bitter if allowed to brown. For a subtle flavor, heat a whole clove of garlic in the oil, then remove it before adding the other ingredients. The flavor of garlic dissipates quite quickly during cooking, so for long-cooked dishes add it toward the end of the cooking time.

Olive (olives)

A wide variety of olives is cultivated all over Italy. Most are destined to be pressed into oil (nearly 20 percent of their weight is oil), but some are kept as table olives to be salted, pickled or marinated, and served as part of an *antipasto* or used in cooking. There are two main types of olive, green (immature) and black (mature); both are bitter and inedible in their natural state. All olives have a high caloric content and are rich in iron, potassium and vitamins.

Green olives are the unripe fruit, which are picked in October or November. They have a sharper flavor and crunchier texture than black olives, which continue to ripen on the tree and are not harvested until December. Among the best Italian table olives are the small, shiny black Gaeta olives from Liguria. Wrinkled black olives from Lazio have a strong, salty flavor, while Sardinian olives are semi-ripened and are brown or purplish in color. The largest olives come from Apulia and Sicily, where giant, green specimens are grown. These are sometimes pitted and stuffed with pimento, anchovy or almonds. Cured olives can be flavored with all sorts of aromatics, such as garlic, local herbs, orange or lemon zest and dried chilies.

HISTORY

Olive trees have been grown in the Mediterranean since Biblical times, when they were brought there from the East by the Romans. Ancient civilizations venerated the olive tree; the Egyptians believed that the goddess Isis discovered the secret of extracting oil from the fruit.

CULINARY USES

Olives can be served on their own or as a garnish or topping for pizza. They are used as an ingredient in many Italian recipes, such as *caponata*. Sicilian *caponata* is a dome-shaped salad of fried eggplants with celery, onions, tomatoes, capers and green olives, while the Ligurian dish of the same name consists of stale crackers or bread soaked in olive oil and topped with a mixture of chopped olives, garlic, anchovies and oregano. Olives combine well with Mediterranean ingredients such as tomatoes, eggplants, anchovies and capers and are used in sauces for rabbit, chicken and firm-fleshed fish. Made into a paste with red wine vinegar, garlic and olive oil, they make an excellent topping for *crostini*.

BUYING AND STORING

Cured olives vary enormously in flavor, so ask to taste one before making your selection. Loose olives can be kept in an airtight container in the refrigerator for up to a week.

Green olives
These unripe olives have a sharper flavor than black olives

Capperi (capers)

Capers are the immature flower buds of a wild Mediterranean shrub. They are pickled in white wine vinegar or preserved in brine, which gives them a piquant, peppery flavor. Sicilian capers are packed in whole salt, which should be rinsed off before using the capers. Bottled nasturtium flower buds are sometimes sold as a cheaper alternative to true capers. Caper berries look like large, fat capers on a long stalk, but they are actually the fruit of the caper shrub. They can be served as an hors d'oeuvre or in a salad.

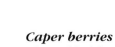

Black olives
Olives are among the oldest fruits known to man. They are grown all over Italy

Caper berries
The pickled fruit of the caper shrub can be served as an hors d'oeuvre.

Herbs & Seasonings

CULINARY USES
Capers are mainly used as a condiment or garnish, but they also add zest to seafood and fish dishes, salads, pizzas and pasta sauces such as the famous Sicilian *pasta colle sarde*, a mixture of sardines, parsley, tomatoes, pine nuts and raisins.

BUYING AND STORING
Choosing pickled or brined capers is a matter of taste, as is whether or not you should rinse them before use. Large capers are usually cheaper than small ones; there is no difference in flavor, but small capers make a more attractive garnish. Salt-packed capers are always sold loose by the *etto* (3½ oz); they should be used as soon as possible. Once opened, jars of capers should be kept in the refrigerator. Make sure any capers left in the jar are covered with the preserving liquid.

Pickled capers
Rinsing these capers before use softens their sharp, piquant flavor

Olio di oliva (olive oil)
Unlike other oils, which are extracted from the seeds or dried fruits of plants, olive oil is pressed from the pulp of ripe olives, which gives it an inimitable richness and flavor. Different regions of Italy produce distinctively different olive oils; Tuscan oil (considered the best) is pungent and peppery, Ligurian oil is lighter and sweeter, while the oils from the south and Sicily are powerful and nutty.

The best olive oil is *extra vergine*, which is strictly controlled and regulated like wine. This is made simply by pressing the olives to extract the oil, with no further processing. Extra virgin olive oil must have an acidity level of less than 1 percent. The distinctive fruity flavor of this oil makes it ideal for dressings and using raw. Virgin olive oil is pressed in the same way, but has a higher acidity level and a less refined flavor. It, too, can be used as a condiment, but is also suitable for cooking. Unclassified olive oil is refined, then blended with virgin oil to add flavor. It has an undistinguished taste, but is ideal for cooking; it should not be used as a condiment.

BUYING AND STORING
The best olive oil comes from Lucca in Tuscany and is very expensive. It is made with slightly under-ripe olives, which give it a luminous green color. If your budget does not stretch to this, buy the best extra virgin oil you can afford to use "neat" or in dressings. Experiment with small bottles of different extra virgin oils to see which you prefer. For cooking, pure olive oil is fine. Once opened, olive oil should be kept in a cool place away from the light. The best oil will soon lose its savor, so use it within six months.

Extra virgin olive oil
The distinctive fruity flavor makes this oil ideal for salad dressings

COOKING WITH OLIVE OIL

Olive oil can be heated to very high temperatures without burning or smoking, which makes it ideal for frying, sauce-making and other cooking. Extra virgin olive oil should be saved for dressing fish, vegetables and salads.

Peperoncini (dried red chilies)

Hot flakes of dried chilies are added to many southern Italian dishes, such as *arrabbiata* sauce and the famous *pasta all'aglio, olio e peperoncino* (dressed with garlic, oil and chilies). Chilies are unusual in that their "hotness" is usually in inverse proportion to their size, so larger dried varieties are generally milder than the smaller ones. In summer, bunches of tiny fresh red chilies can be bought in Italian markets. These can be used fresh, preserved in olive oil to make a spicy dressing or to drizzle over a pizza, or hung up to dry and crumbled to add "oomph" to a dish. Crushed chili flakes are available in jars.

CULINARY USES

A small pinch of dried chili flakes spices up stews and sauces, particularly those made with tomatoes. For a really hot pizza, crumble a few flakes over the top. Dried chilies are extremely fiery and should be used very sparingly.

BUYING AND STORING

Dried chilies will last for years, but they do lose their savor over a period of time, so buy only small quantities. Whole *peperoncini* should be hung up in bunches and crumbled directly into the dish you are cooking.

Zafferano (saffron)

Saffron consists of the dried stigmas of the saffron crocus. It takes about 80,000 crocuses to produce about 1¼ lb of spice and these have to be hand-picked, so it is hardly surprising that saffron is the world's most expensive spice. Saffron stigmas or threads are a vivid orangey-red color with a pungent aroma. They are also sold ground into powder. Saffron has a highly aromatic flavor and will impart a wonderful, rich golden color to risotti and sauces.

Dried chilies
These are often used in fiery southern Italian dishes, such as arrabbiata *sauce*

Dried red chili flakes
Just a small pinch of these fiery flakes spices up stews and sauces

Saffron threads
Used to flavor and color the classic risotto alla milanese

HISTORY

Saffron originated in Asia Minor, where it was used by ancient civilizations as a flavoring, as a dye, in perfumery and for medicinal purposes. Arab traders brought the spice to the Mediterranean in the tenth century; for centuries it was so highly prized that stealing or adulterating it was punishable by death. The best saffron is nowadays cultivated in Spain, but it is also grown in Italy.

CULINARY USES

In Italy, saffron is mainly used to flavor and color risotti, such as the classic *risotto alla milanese*. It is excellent in sauces for fish and poultry and can be used to flavor cookies and cakes.

BUYING AND STORING

Saffron threads are sold in small boxes or jars containing only a few strands. The wiry threads should be a deep orangey-red in color; paler yellowish-orange threads are probably the much cheaper and less desirable safflower, which will add color but not flavor to a dish. Powdered saffron is convenient to use, but less reliable, as it may have been adulterated with safflower. Stored in small, airtight containers, saffron will keep for months.

COOKING WITH SAFFRON

Do not add saffron directly to a dish. Infuse threads in a little hot water for at least 5 minutes before blending into a dish to bring out the flavor and ensure even coloring. Add the soaking water together with the threads. Never fry saffron in hot oil or butter; this will ruin the flavor.

Cakes, Cookies & Breads

In Italy it is perfectly normal and acceptable for a hostess to buy a dolce *(cake or dessert) to serve at the end of a meal, rather than make it herself. Pastry shops and bakeries sell a wide variety of traditional tarts, spiced yeast cakes and cookies to be enjoyed with coffee or a glass of vin santo, sweet dessert wine or a liqueur. Some of these, such as* panettone *and* colomba, *are reserved for special occasions like Christmas and Easter, and almost every town has its own specialty for its local saint's day.*

Amaretti (macaroons)

Amaretti cookies are made from ground almonds, egg whites and sugar. They have a distinctive flavor, which comes from the addition of bitter almonds. They originated in Venice during the Renaissance and their English name of macaroons comes from the Venetian *macerone*, meaning "fine paste." They come in dozens of different forms, from the famous crunchy sugar-encrusted cookies wrapped in pairs in twists of crisp white paper to soft-centered macaroons wrapped in brightly-colored foil. Amaretti are delicious dipped into hot coffee. They can also be crumbled to make a stuffing for baked peaches or apricots.

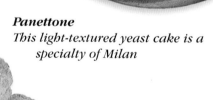

Panettone
This light-textured yeast cake is a specialty of Milan

Cantucci

These hard, high-baked lozenge-shaped cookies from Tuscany are designed to be dipped into *espresso* coffee or vin santo. When moistened, they become deliciously soft and crumbly. They are usually studded with almonds or other nuts and flavored with aniseed or vanilla.

Cantucci

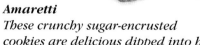

Amaretti
These crunchy sugar-encrusted cookies are delicious dipped into hot coffee

Panettone

Literally meaning "big bread," *panettone* is a light-textured spiced yeast bread containing raisins and candied fruit. Originally a specialty of Milan, it is now sold all over Italy as a Christmas delicacy and is traditionally given as a gift. *Panettoni* can vary in size from small to enormous. They are sometimes sold in pastel-colored dome-shaped boxes, which are often hung from the ceiling of bakeries and delicatessens, and look very festive. At Easter, they are baked into the shape of a lamb (*agnello*) or a dove (*colomba*). *Panettone* is sliced into wedges and eaten like cake.

Crumiri

These sweet elbow-shaped cookies are a speciality of Piedmont. The rich golden brown dough is made with polenta and honey and piped through a fluted nozzle to give the cookies their characteristic ridged texture. Although the cookies seem hard on the outside, the polenta flour gives the *crumiri* a pleasantly crunchy texture. *Crumiri* are good snack cookies, but they are also excellent dipped in hot coffee.

Panforte

Somewhat resembling a Christmas pudding in flavor, but shaped like a flat disc, *panforte* is a rich, dark spiced cake crammed with dried fruit and toasted nuts. It is a speciality of Siena and is sold in a colorful glossy wrapping, often depicting Sienese scenes. It is extremely rich, so can only be eaten in small quantities, which is just as well, since it is also quite expensive.

Panettone
The characteristic box often hangs from the ceiling in Italian delicatessens

Panforte
This Italian spice cake is packed full of fruit and nuts

Savoiardi
These soft-textured, Italian sponge finger cookies are used as a base for tiramisù

Savoiardi (sponge cookies)

As their name suggests, *savoiardi* come from the Savoy region of Piedmont. They are plumper and wider than sponge fingers and have a softer texture. They are excellent dunked into tea or coffee, and are traditionally served with *zabaglione*; but they are best of all used as a base for tiramisù, the wickedly rich Italian coffee and mascarpone dessert.

Pane (Bread)

No Italian meal is ever served without bread to accompany the food. Indeed, it often constitutes one of the dishes in a meal in the form of *crostini* and *bruschetta* (toasted canapés), soups such as *pancotto*, *panzanella* (bread salad) or pizza. In Tuscany, bread plays a more important part in the food of the region than pasta. A favorite antipasto is *fettunta*, toasted or grilled bread rubbed with garlic, anointed with plenty of olive oil and sprinkled with coarse salt. When a topping is added, it becomes *bruschetta*.

Italians buy or make fresh bread every day, but stale or leftover loaves are never wasted. Instead they are made into bread crumbs and used for thickening sauces and stews, or for stuffings, salads or wonderfully sustaining soups.

There are hundreds of different types of Italian bread with many regional variations to suit the local food. Traditional Tuscan country bread is made without salt, since it is designed to be served with salty cured meats such as salami and *prosciutto crudo*. (If you prefer salted bread, ask for *pane salato*.) Southern Italian breads often contain olive oil, which goes well with tomatoes. *Pane integrale* (whole-wheat bread) is traditionally baked in a wood oven. The texture and flavor of the bread depends on the type of flour used and the amount of seasoning, but nearly all Italian breads are firm-textured with substantial crusts. You will never find flabby damp white sandwich loaves in an Italian bakery, although the inside of traditional white *panini* (bread rolls) can sometimes resemble cotton balls.

Ciabatta

These flattish, slipper-shaped loaves with squared or rounded ends are made with olive oil and are often flavored with fresh or dried herbs, olives or sun-dried tomatoes. They have an airy texture inside and a pale, crisp crust. *Ciabatta* is delicious served warm, and is excellent for sandwiches.

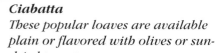

Ciabatta
These popular loaves are available plain or flavored with olives or sun-dried tomatoes

Whole-wheat bread
In Italy this bread is traditionally baked in a wooden oven

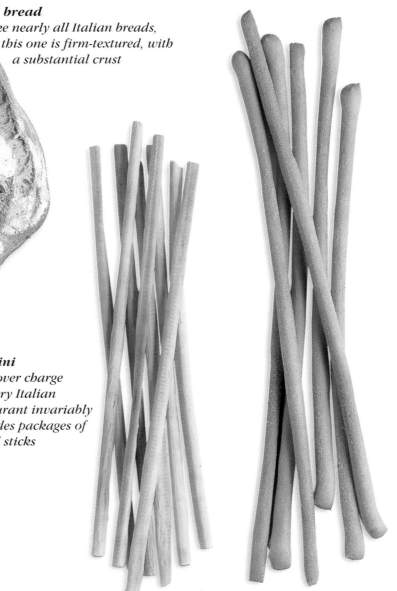

Focaccia

A dimpled flat bread similar to pizza dough, *focaccia* is traditionally oiled and baked in a wood oven. A whole *focaccia* from a bakery weighs several pounds and is sold by weight, cut into manageable pieces. A variety of ingredients can be worked into the dough or serve as a topping— onions, *pancetta*, rosemary or oregano, ham, cheese or olives. *Focaccine* are small versions, which are split and served with fillings like a sandwich. In Apulia, *focaccia del Venerdì Santo*, with its topping of fennel, chicory, anchovies, olives and capers, is traditionally served on Good Friday.

Focaccia
In Italy these large flat breads are sold by weight, cut into manageable pieces. It can be plain, as here, or flavored with herbs, sun-dried tomatoes or olives

White bread
Like nearly all Italian breads, this one is firm-textured, with a substantial crust

Grissini
The cover charge in every Italian restaurant invariably includes packages of bread sticks

Grissini

These crisp golden bread sticks originated in Turin, but are now found in almost every Italian restaurant, packaged in long envelopes. They range in size from matchstick-thin to hefty, knobby, homemade batons. Italian bakers often use up any leftover dough to make *grissini*, which are sold loose by weight. They can be rolled in sesame or poppy seeds for extra flavor.

Pantry

One of the great joys of Italian food is that you can create a delicious meal almost instantly using ingredients from your pantry. Rice and pasta can be combined with any number of jarred or canned vegetables, seafood or sauces to make a speedy and nutritious meal. Unopened jars and cans last for months, if not years, so it is worth keeping a selection in your pantry for an impromptu meal that you can create in moments.

Pesto

Although nothing is as good as homemade pesto, there are some excellent jarred varieties of this fragrant green basil sauce. Traditional pesto is made with basil, pine nuts, Parmesan or Pecorino cheese and olive oil, but you may also find a red version based on red bell peppers.

CULINARY USES

Pesto can be used as an instant dressing for any type of pasta or potato gnocchi. It gives a lift to risotti and tomato sauces, and is delicious stirred into minestrone or tomato-based soups. A spoonful of pesto will add a new dimension to bottled mayonnaise, creating a rich, pungent *maionese verde*. For a quick, attractive hors d'oeuvre, halve some cherry tomatoes, scoop out the seeds and fill the tomatoes with pesto.

Pesto
Both the traditional green version shown here and a red type based on red bell peppers are used to flavor sauces and pasta

Pomodori secchi (sun-dried tomatoes)

Sun-drying tomatoes intensifies their flavor to an astonishing sweetness and pungency and allows you to enjoy the full savor of tomatoes even in winter. If you are extremely lucky, you may still find in markets in southern Italy locally grown tomatoes that have been spread out to dry in the sun, but the commercially produced "sun-dried" tomatoes are actually air-dried by machine. Wrinkled red dried tomatoes are available dry in packages or preserved in olive oil. Dry tomatoes are brick-red in color and have a chewy texture. They can be eaten on their own as a snack, but for cooking they should be soaked in hot water until soft (the tomato-flavored soaking water can be used for a soup or sauce). Jarred sun-dried tomatoes are sold in chunky pieces or as a paste.

Dried tomatoes
Dried tomatoes should always be softened in water before use

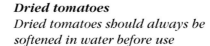

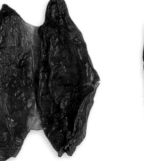 

Sun-dried tomatoes
These strong-flavored tomatoes add extra piquancy to dishes

CULINARY USES

Sun-dried tomatoes add piquancy to vegetable dishes, soups or sauces. They can be chopped and added to a simple *sugo di pomodoro* or a meaty *ragù* for extra flavor. They make an excellent *antipasto* combined with sliced fresh tomatoes, mozzarella and basil or with other preserved or pickled vegetables. They go well with fresh Mediterranean vegetables like fennel, eggplants and zucchini, and add a special something to egg dishes, such as *frittata*. Use the oil in which the tomatoes are preserved for salad dressings or for sweating vegetables for a soup or sauce.

The paste can be used in small quantities for sauces and soups, or used on its own or with a little butter as a dressing for pasta.

**Black
olive paste**

Legumi sott'olio *(vegetables preserved in oil)*

Italians produce a wide variety of vegetables preserved in olive or sunflower oil, or a mixture of both. The choicest are often cooked *alla brace* (grilled) before being packed in the best olive oil—tiny *carciofini* (artichokes), *funghi* and *porcini* (button and wild mushrooms), *peperoni* (red and yellow bell peppers) and *melanzane* (eggplants)—and look as beautiful as they taste. You will sometimes find large bulbous jars containing colorful layers of different vegetables in oil; these are packed by hand and are extremely expensive.

CULINARY USES

A mixture of oil-preserved vegetables combined with a selection of cured meats makes a wonderful *antipasto*. They can also be chopped or sliced and used to dress hot or cold pasta, or stirred into rice for a substantial cold salad. They make a delicious topping for *crostini* or pizza.

Passata
This rich tomato pureé varies in fineness from the ultra-smooth to the chunkier sugocasa

**Green
olive paste**

Passata *(tomato pulp)*

Rich red passata is simply sieved ripe tomatoes, a wonderfully convenient shortcut whenever tomato pulp is required. Depending on the degree of sieving, it can be perfectly smooth or slightly chunky (*polpa di pomodoro* or *passata rustica*: "rustic passata"). The chunky variety is sold in tall jars, while the smoothest type is available in cartons or jars. More highly concentrated tomato paste (*concentrato di pomodoro*) is packed in small cans or tubes. This product is extremely strong and should only be used in small quantities.

CULINARY USES

Passata can be used as a basis for soups and sauces, and as a substitute for fresh tomatoes in all recipes where they require long cooking. For a very quick pasta sauce, sweat some finely chopped onion and garlic in olive oil, add a jar of passata and bubble the sauce while the pasta is cooking. Flavor with fresh basil, oregano, parsley or some chopped olives, capers and/or anchovies. For more body and depth and a richer color, stir in a spoonful or two of tomato concentrate.

Pasta di olive *(olive paste)*

Green or, more usually, black olives are pounded to a paste with salt and olive oil and packed in small jars. Olive paste tends to be very salty and rich, so a little goes a long way.

CULINARY USES

Olive paste can be spread very thinly over pizza bases, or scraped onto toasted croutons and topped with tomatoes or mushrooms to make *crostini*. Mixed with olive oil and a little lemon juice, it can be a dip for raw vegetables. For an interesting *antipasto*, mash a little olive paste into the yolks of halved hard-cooked eggs, spoon the mixture back into the cavity and top with a few capers.

A little olive paste adds a rich flavor to a tomato sauce, while a spoonful stirred into a vinaigrette makes a good dressing for a robust salad. If you are a real olive lover, stir a small amount into hot pasta for the simplest of dressings.

Artichoke hearts
These olive oil-packed vegetables are often combined with sliced cured meats to make an antipasto

Pantry

Giardiniera (pickled vegetables)

Mixed pickled vegetables are sold packed *in agrodolce* (vinegar and oil). Single varieties such as peeled or unpeeled eggplants and zucchini are available, but a mixture of these vegetables along with artichokes, baby onions, carrots, celery and peppers is more colorful. These vegetables are sometimes described as *alla contadina* (peasant-style).

CULINARY USES

Pickled vegetables can be served with salami and ham as an *antipasto*, or drained and mixed with raw vegetables and mayonnaise for a piquant version of *insalata russa* (Russian salad). Their vinegary taste makes an excellent counterpoint to plain cold roast meats or poultry.

Peppers
The vinegary flavor of these pickled vegetables goes well with cold roast meats

Filetti di acciughe (anchovy fillets)

Anchovy fillets are available preserved in salt or oil. The salted fillets have a superior flavor, but they are are only available in catering tins to be sold by the *etto* (3½ oz) at delicatessens. You can buy these and soak them for 30 minutes, then dry them thoroughly and pack them in olive oil, but it is more practical to buy canned or jarred anchovies.

CULINARY USES

Anchovies can be chopped and added to tomato sauces and salad dressings. They can be stirred into a fish risotto, or mixed with tomatoes and capers for a topping for pizzas or *crostini*. They are best of all made into *bagna cauda*, a delicious and quick hot dip for raw vegetables. For six people, heat ⅔ cup olive oil with 4 tbsp unsalted butter. As soon as it begins to foam, add 3 finely chopped garlic cloves and soften but do not brown. Drain and roughly chop a 2-oz can of anchovy fillets, add to the pan and stir over low heat until they have disintegrated to a paste. Keep the sauce hot and dip in the vegetables.

Anchovy fillets
Usually chopped and added to sauces or salads for extra flavor. These are available packed in oil or salt—the salted variety have a better flavor

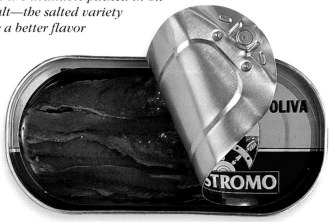

Bottarga (salted roe)

The pressed, salted and dried roe of the gray mullet or tuna, also known as *buttariga, butarega* and *ovotarica*, is a speciality of Sardinia, Sicily and the Veneto, where it is regarded as a great delicacy. It is usually packed in a sausage shape inside a skin that should be removed before preparing. Wrapped in plastic wrap, it will keep for several months.

CULINARY USES

Bottarga can be served as an *antipasto* thinly sliced and dressed with a little extra virgin olive oil and lemon juice. In Sicily, it is served with *caponata*, a dome-shaped salad of fried eggplant and celery. It is delicious simply grated over hot pasta with a pat of unsalted butter and a little chopped fresh parsley or dried chili flakes.

Baccalà (salted dried cod)

Air-drying is the oldest known method of preserving fish. Before the days of deep-freezing, dried fish was invaluable for people who wished to observe meatless days, but who lived far from the sea, because the salting and drying process ensures that it remains edible for many months. The most popular dried fish in Italy is salt cod, which is traditionally eaten on Good Friday. It is sometimes known confusingly as *stoccafisso* (although true stockfish is unsalted). It looks rather unappealing, like a flat, grayish board, but once it has been soaked and reconstituted it is absolutely delicious. Unlike other pantry ingredients, *baccalà* must be prepared a day in advance, but it is worth the effort.

Clams in brine

Salt cod
This is the favorite Italian dried fish—it looks unappealing, but once it is soaked and cooked, it is delicious

CULINARY USES
Before using *baccalà*, it must be soaked under cold running water for at least 8 hours to rehydrate it and remove the excess salt. Once this has been done, it can be creamed with olive oil, garlic, cream and parsley to make *baccalà mantecato*, a famous Venetian dish, which is served on fried polenta. In the Florentine version, the salt cod is cut into chunks, coated with flour and fried with tomatoes and onions. *Baccalà* combines well with all Mediterranean flavors and can be stewed or baked with red bell peppers, potatoes, fennel or celery, capers, olives and anchovies. Many recipes also include pine nuts and raisins. For a simple pasta sauce, mix some flaked salt cod with cream and chopped herbs and stir it into the hot pasta.

Vongole (clams)

Tiny clams are sold packed in brine in glass jars. These miniature golden nuggets need no further cooking and can be simply heated through and tossed into hot pasta or risotto, or combined with tomato sauce. If you have time, drain the clams and reduce the juice in which they are packed with finely chopped garlic and a few dried chili flakes to make a more intense sauce.

Mostarda di Cremona (mustard fruit chutney)

This sweet crystallized fruit chutney with its piquant undertone of the mustard was first produced over a hundred years ago in Cremona and Venice. Its vibrant colors come from the assortment of candied fruits from which it is made—cherries, pears, melons, figs, apricots and clementines, infused in mustard seed oil. Also known as *mostarda di frutta*, the chutney is traditionally served with sausages such as zampone and cotechino, or roast and boiled beef, veal and pork. For an unusual and delicious dessert, serve the chutney as a topping for creamy mascarpone.

Mustard fruit chutney

Aperitifs & Liqueurs

Behind every bar in Italy is displayed row upon row of bottles containing dozens of different aperitivi *and* digestivi, *many of them never found outside Italy. They are consumed at any hour of the day; a favorite Italian morning drink is* caffè corretto, *espresso coffee laced with grappa or Stock (Italian brandy). Many of the vermouths and spirits are made from local ingredients, including herbs, nuts, lemons, artichokes or regional wines. The Italians have an unshakeable belief in the digestive properties of such drinks, many of which are so bitter that most non-Italians find them completely unpalatable. At the end of a restaurant meal, you will always find the men clustered around the bar aiding their digestion with a small glass of spirit or liqueur.*

Amaro

A very bitter *aperitivo* much beloved by the Italians, *amaro* is flavored with gentian, herbs and orange peel and contains quinine and iron. Marginally less bitter than straight *amaro* are the wine-based *amari* such as Campari, which is usually mixed with soda water and drunk before a meal to stimulate the appetite and cleanse the palate. Others, such as Fernet-Branca, are served as a pick-me-up and cure for stomach aches. *Amaro* is reputed to have excellent digestive and tonic properties, to cure hangovers and to have aphrodisiac qualities, which probably explains its popularity in Italy.

Campari

A bright crimson *aperitivo* from the *amaro* family, wine-based Campari has a bitter, astringent flavor. It was first produced in the nineteenth century by the Campari brothers from Milan, and has been produced by the same family ever since. Campari is sold in triangular single-portion bottles ready-mixed with soda (Campari soda). The neat bitters are an essential ingredient of cocktails such as *Negroni* and *Americano*.

Amaro

Fernet-Branca

Campari soda

Cynar

This dark brown, intensely bitter, aperitif with an alcoholic content of 17 percent is made from artichokes. Too bitter to swallow on its own, it is usually served as a long drink with ice and soda water.

Punt e Mes

The name of this intensely bitter red *aperitivo* means "point and a half." It is said to have been created by the Carpano distillery when customers ordered their drinks to be mixed according to their own specification. Punt e Mes is usually drunk on its own, but can be served with ice and soda.

Vermouth

All vermouths, both white and red, are made from white wine flavored with aromatic herbal extracts and spices. The first vermouth was made in Turin in the eighteenth century, and vermouth is still produced there. Red vermouths, such as Cinzano and sweet Martini, are sweetened with sugar and tinted with caramel to give them a deep red color. These sweet red varieties are generically called "Italian" vermouth—the "it" in gin and it. Dry vermouth is white and contains less sugar. It is known as "French," but is also produced in Italy by companies such as Martini and Rossi. Other well-known brands include Riccadonna and Gancia.

CULINARY USES

Although the Italians tend to use white wine rather than vermouth in their cooking, dry white vermouth can be substituted in sauces and veal, rabbit or poultry dishes. It adds a touch of dryness and intensity.

Cynar

Punt e Mes

Extra-dry white vermouth

Fortified Wines

Marsala

This rich brown fortified wine has a sweet, musky flavor and an alcoholic content of about 18 percent. It is made in the west of Sicily, near the town from which it takes its name. The best Marsala (*vergine*) has been matured for at least five years to give an intensity of flavor and color. Although sweet Marsala is better known, dry varieties (*ambra secco*) are also produced; their flavor is reminiscent of medium sherry. The sweetest version is *Marsala all'uovo*, an intensely rich and sticky dessert wine enriched with egg yolks, which can only be drunk in tiny quantities. Dry Marsala is generally served as an *aperitivo*, while the sweet version is served after a meal, usually with little cookies to dip into the wine. Unlike sherry, sweet Marsala does not deteriorate once the bottle is opened, so it makes a very useful standby in the kitchen.

Vin santo

This "holy wine" from Tuscany is made from semi-dried grapes with a long slow fermentation, followed by many years of aging to produce a syrupy golden wine. Although not a fortified wine, its intense flavor has some similarity to sherry and it is drunk in much the same way. Vin santo can be dry or sweet, but the sweet version is more common. It is generally served with a plate of *cantucci* or *biscotti di Prato*, hard slipper-shaped cookies studded with nuts. These are dunked into the wine to make a delicious dessert.

Vin santo

CULINARY USES

Sweet Marsala is probably best known as an essential ingredient of *zabaglione*, a light frothy dessert made from whisked egg yolks, sugar and Marsala. It is used in *zuppa inglese* (trifle) and many other desserts. Dry Marsala is widely used in Italian cooking, particularly in veal dishes such as *scaloppina* and *piccata al Marsala* and sautéed chicken livers. A few spoonfuls of Marsala added to the pan in which veal or poultry has been sautéed will mingle with the pan juices to make a delicious syrupy sauce. It adds extra flavor to wild mushrooms or a mushroom risotto.

Marsala
The sweet variety is used to flavor zabaglione

Marsala
Widely used by Italian cooks for flavoring veal and poultry dishes

Liqueurs & Digestivi

Amaretto

This sweet liqueur is made from apricot pits and flavored with almonds and aromatic extracts. There are several brands produced, but the best is Disaronno Amaretto, which comes in a distinctive squarish rippled glass bottle with a square cap.

Culinary Uses

The distinctive almond flavor of Amaretto enhances many desserts, such as *macedonia* (fruit salad), *zuppa inglese* (trifle) and *panna* (whipped cream).

Galliano

A bright yellow liqueur from Lombardy, Galliano is flavored with herbs and spices and tastes a little like a bittersweet Chartreuse. It is occasionally drunk on its own as a *digestivo*, but is best known as an ingredient for cocktails such as Harvey Wallbanger and Golden Cadillac.

Galliano

Amaretto

Grappa

A pungent colorless brandy with an alcoholic content of about 40 percent, distilled from the pressed skins and seeds of the grapes left after wine-making. At its crudest, grappa tastes of raw spirit, but after maturing the taste becomes refined and the best grappa can be as good as a fine French *marc*. Grappa is made in many regions, usually from local grapes, which lend each variety its characteristic flavor. On the whole, you get what you pay for; cheap grappa is fiery and pungent, while expensive, well-matured varieties can be very smooth. The very best grappa often comes in exquisite hand-blown bottles. The spirit can be flavored with various aromatics, including rose petals and lemon peel.

CULINARY USES

Grappa is not used in Italian cooking, except in *capretto alla piemontese* (braised goat). It can be used for flambéeing and for preserving berries. The spirit takes on the flavor of the berries and can be drunk as a *digestivo* after the berries have been eaten.

Liquore al limone or Cedro

This sticky sweet liqueur is made from the peel of the lemons that grow in profusion around the Amalfi coast. Almost every delicatessen in the region sells a homemade version of this opaque yellow drink, whose sweetness is tempered by the tangy citrus fruit. It should be served ice-cold straight from the refrigerator or freezer and makes a refreshing *aperitivo* or *digestivo*.

Liquore al limone

Maraschino

This sweet, colorless cherry liqueur is made from fermented bitter Maraschino cherries. It can be drunk on its own as a *digestivo*, but is more commonly used for flavoring cocktails or sweet dishes.

Maraschino

Grappa

Nocino

This sticky, dark brown liqueur from Emilia-Romagna is made from unripe green walnuts steeped in spirit. It has an aromatic but bittersweet flavor.

Sambuca

The colorless liqueur has a strong taste of aniseed, although it is actually distilled from witch elder. Traditionally it is served in a schooner-shaped glass, flambéed and with a coffee bean floating on top. The coffee bean is crunched as the Sambuca is drunk, so that its bitterness counteracts the intense sweetness of the liqueur. This method of serving Sambuca is known as *colla mosca* ("with the fly"), the "fly" being the coffee bean.

Strega

A bright yellow liqueur made from herbs and flowers, strega (meaning "witch"), has a bittersweet flavor and is definitely an acquired taste.

Nocino

Sambuca

Strega

Index

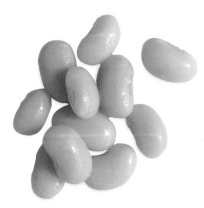

Index

Index